JILTED

Lisa Handy-Tunsil
Jilted

Published by BooxAi

ISBN: 978-965-577-963-9

JILTED

EMBRACING NEW LIFE

LISA HANDY-TUNSIL

I dedicate this book to my children, Kenitra Middleton and Kenneth Middleton II, and to my beautiful nieces Davione & Da'Ja, who I love as my own. I hope this book gives you the courage to face any of life's obstacles, knowing with God's help you can get through anything. I pray that my life will continually be an example to you all. I love you!

Daddy, I dedicate this book to you as well. You're gone but never forgotten. You may not be here to see this book come to manifestation, but I'm thankful that you had the chance to hear it since the baby brat my sister (Yolanda) read you many chapters as I was writing it. You already considered me a great speaker and writer ahead of time. When I didn't understand the things that were going on after Ken's death, you were there to guide me and encourage me. You reminded me that God's timing isn't our timing and that he was blessing me for my love, commitment, and loyalty. I miss you and love you. Your memory will forever live on through me.

CONTENTS

FOREWORD

Unresolved grief keeps individuals on pause. It truly slows everything in your life down when it is not dealt with effectively and properly. Many books and guides have been written on grief recovery to help those experiencing overwhelming situations. I have dealt with an array of predicaments that could have isolated me in the box of grief; deaths, broken relationships, missed opportunities, self-sabotage, etc. I had to make a conscious decision that I did not want to stay there and become open to a healing process.

The (title) is a life-changing resource that will challenge you to be open, honest, and ready for lasting recovery. One of the truths from Lisa's writings that confirm the impact of this guide is that you can have every resource and even God, but without your Full Participation, there will be no progress.

The pages of this guide will equip, empower, and give you the spiritual and natural strategies to live as you get through grief. Lisa writes from a personal, professional, and spiritual perspective that is reliable, relatable, enjoyable, and easy read to comprehend.

Whether you are in the beginning stages of grief, intermediate, or have been dealing with grief for a long time, this guide will assist you on your journey to living a whole life despite what you've been through.

TaSheekia Harris
Founder of Crowning Daughters for Success Enrichment Program,
Author of Dressing Mu Inner Beauty and Protect Your Pearls Dating
Guide

INTRODUCTION

In life, we're often faced with a life-changing experience. It's nothing we asked for, neither is it something we could have ever imagined. At times we are blind-sided by many of the life events we are faced with in our lifetime. Suddenly being thrown into the reality of losing a loved one left me with a pain that I wouldn't wish on anyone. It's indescribable and it's like nothing I've ever experienced before.

One of the definitions of grief is to suffer disappointment, misfortune, or other trouble or to fail at something. That definition doesn't begin to scratch the surface of how grief really makes one feel, think, or even act. All I know is that my heart was severely wounded, opened, or cut without any type of medicine to cure it or at the least stop the pain.

Moving forward didn't happen by chance or accident. It required my full participation. Sometimes we sit back and tell God to deliver or heal us and we think he's going to drop down and do just that. We must remember God gives us many avenues to help us through life. We sometimes miss them because we won't open ourselves up and allow the healing process to begin.

I had to decide this didn't come because I was bad or because God wanted to punish me. Sometimes in life, we will never get all of the answers we seek, but we can become better and stronger once we go through the process. I decided I wanted to LIVE life to the fullest and not just exist because there is a big difference.

This book is not intended to exalt grief but to help you gain power over it. To let you know that your heart can be healed. Just open up your heart and mind to be enlightened and to know that grief has no power over you unless you continue to allow it to. You can move forward and embrace your new chapter. As you begin to read this book, my prayer for you is that while you're reading, God's healing power will begin to overtake you. Just open up your heart and mind to receive the healing that's waiting for you.

You must be INTENTIONAL!

CHAPTER ONE

OUR HAPPY HOME

It began when we were in high school looking across our science classroom at one another. Ken and I shared glances without any conversations for a while, and we eventually developed a friendship where we admired one another. Every day he found an excuse to sit by me or find an excuse to strike up a conversation with me. We became best of friends and talked every day in class, but we never talked outside of school.

I would long for the next day just to see Ken's magnetic smile. I thought I only liked him as a friend, but there was something I saw in this little skinny boy that drew me to him. He was funny, well-dressed, and responsible all at the same time. Ken became known as the class clown because he made us laugh every day, including the teachers. I saw a young boy standing before me. I could see he would grow into a man with a purpose.

Every day we waited for each other so that we could sit next to or close to each other, but neither of us said a word about it. I believe he liked me, and what he saw, but I dared not say a word because I was raised to let the boy do the chasing. Instead of asking me for my phone number, Ken pretended to take magazine subscriptions that required a phone number, so what else could I do but buy a subscription so he could call me?.. We talked that evening, and our first conversation outside of school led to phone calls every night getting to know each other.

Time passed, but we never spoke a word of our feelings for one another even though we enjoyed each other's company daily. He often dropped hints to let me know he liked me, but I couldn't respond to him because if I opened my mouth, he would have known he was attracting more of my heart each day. I just enjoyed being around him. He had such a radiant smile and it was contagious, making everyone around him smile.

The day finally came when the ice broke. Every year our high school held a dress-up day. Who knew Ken and I would come to school dressed just alike? We didn't!. We wore white dress shirts with black dress pants, and we looked good. Ken looked across the room at me and could no longer hold his thoughts inside.

His eyes lit up as he walked toward me and said, "You look good."

At this point, I had to break down and say, "Boy, you look good yourself."

He then told me that I looked so good, so he was going to let me take a picture with him as if he were this big celebrity. Lol! This was a plot so he would have an excuse to put his arms around me, and I didn't mind at all. Our classmates asked if we planned this and he was such a clown. He knew exactly how to respond with just a grin. I, on the other hand, saw this as an opportunity to stake my claim. For every girl who asked if we planned this, I smiled as if to say yes. I wanted them to know he was mine.

He realized I allowed the girls to think we planned this, and he looked at me with his little sly grin and said, "Oh, we planned this, hah?" I smiled back and said, of course, and we both knew we had silently given each other our hearts.

Ken told me to eat lunch with him that day and we ate, laughed, and just enjoyed one another. After school, he drove me and told me that because I looked so good, he would let me hang out with him and pick me up for school the next morning. Who was I to disappoint him? I realized that was Ken's way of staking his claim to me as well.

I waited with excitement for the sound of his car. He picked me up for school and picked me up from work but never did ask if I would go out with him. He just said things like he would pick me up for the game. I guess he knew the attraction was mutual, so we just flowed with it.

I couldn't stop thinking about him. While in my classes I had to talk to myself just to stop daydreaming about us. By this time, we both were seniors, so this was no time to mess up my grades. It was hard trying not to think about him, hoping the bell would hurry up and ring so I could meet him at my locker, where we always met up between classes.

We were two kids in love and didn't care that our friends and family told us not to get too serious because we were too young. We just went with the feelings of our hearts.

May of 1983 arrived and it was graduation time. We were marched down the aisles in our caps and gowns, but Ken and I weren't alone. We were expecting our first child. I was scared and uncertain about my future, but I knew that every decision I made now involved putting our bundle of joy first.

Having a baby on the way never stopped our fun. We went on daily walks to the store to fulfill my cravings, spent time at the beach and the movies. We wanted the world to know we were in love and it didn't care if anyone thought we were too young. We knew what we had was real

Having a baby just out of high school changed our plans. I put college in the back seat.

We continued having fun and still went to the beach and literally raced up and down the beach, and we wrestled each other until we were tired. Now his mother didn't like us playing and running because I was pregnant and she wanted me to be careful. He would try to tell her that he tried to stop me from running and moving about, but he knew this was what I loved to do. Our fun and free spirit were just how who we were.

In August of 1983, we got engaged. It wasn't because he asked me to marry him. We had gone to dinner one weekend and it was near a jewelry store, so we decided to go and look in the store. He asked me if I liked a particular ring and I just said yes without even looking at it, because I was more interested in the beautiful necklaces. I never wanted to talk about marriage even though I knew that I loved him. I never wanted us to marry just because I was pregnant.

On the following Monday, after getting in, he told me to look in his drawer and get something for him, and when I opened it, there was a box sitting inside, and I pulled it out to give to him. His response was to open the box. I opened the box to find my engagement ring in there, and he just simply said: "Put that on. It's yours." (So much for romance and proposing) LOL!

We got married the same year we graduated high school on December 2nd, 1983. I was 18 and he was 19 years old. The fun was still in our lives. Although I was pregnant, we still walked and talked and went to the beach, which was my favorite spot at the time. We did this right up until it was time for the baby to be born.

Although having a few scares along the way with the possibility of a miscarriage at times, I started to have labor pains on a Tuesday afternoon. They were 12-15 minutes apart the whole day. Ken worked a little late that day, so he didn't get home sometimes until around 8:00 pm. I told him about the pains, and his tiredness turned into excitement. I told him to go ahead and eat and rest because I knew we had a while before I would go to the hospital. I knew the pains had to be a lot closer than they were.

Around 11:30 pm the pains were about 5-6 minutes apart, and he was ready to go to the hospital. I forgot to mention prior to these events, he always talked about how he would speed to the hospital so he could have a police escort so that he could have an exciting story to tell. The labor pains were coming closer and harder so off to the hospital we went. He tried so hard to get a police escort by speeding to the hospital, but there were no cops in sight. Normally prior to my labor, there would always be cops to assist him when they stopped him for speeding. LOL!

I had a long hard labor and the doctors told him to walk me around so that I would dilate more. He took great pleasure in walking me swiftly up and down the aisles of that hospital, so I could hurry up and deliver, but somehow this didn't work.

Every time I would go back to the room to be checked to see if I had dilated more, it would only be a half of a centimeter. Low and behold Ken came up with a plan. The next sign I saw said stairs and I tried to pull away while laughing at the same time. I said I know you have lost your mind if you think I'm going up and down those stairs with all of this belly, but I couldn't pull away. He just simply looked at me and smiled and said, come on, I promise I won't let you fall, and this will make you dilate more, and here I go listening to him again and up and down the stairs. I went while laughing and thinking to myself; only my husband would think of this.

You see, this was the kind of guy he was. Always able to do something goofy to make me laugh or just to try something different, but it worked. This time when I returned to my room, I was ready to push. Here goes the comedian holding my hand and every time he saw that I was having another contraction, he would say, "Sweetheart, how many more babies are we going to have?" I looked at him, rolled my eyes, and told him if he didn't stop making jokes, I was going to have them to put him out, but of course, I wasn't about to do that. The laughter made me tolerate the labor pains really well.

It's now the next day (Wednesday) at 6:38pm (long hah). Here comes our 7'3 oz baby girl, who put a gleam of joy in our eyes. He just held her and looked as if someone had given him a million dollars. I had to make him let me hold our daughter because he was acting as if he did all of the hard work. She was a daddy's girl from the moment she entered this world. She was in love with him instantly and he loved her dearly.

Three and a half years passed and we were in love again with our brand new 7'0 lb. baby boy, who entered the scene and brought so much joy to our lives. We now had the perfect set, one girl and one boy. Now this one instantly fell in love with his mother. He looked in my face with a big smile, but once again, I still had to demand to hold him because his dad wanted to take all of the credit once again. LOL!!! He was the proud father of two, and he wanted to show them off to the world.

Over the years they brought us much joy. We always took family trips together and spent much quality time together as a family. We both were there for every dance recital, cheerleader competition, or whatever it was his little girl decided she wanted to participate in. He not only was there for all of our son's sports events, but he would also help coach his football team and his basketball team. We were always a close-knit family who was very present in our children's lives.

We grew with our kids, always encouraging them to be the best they can be in life, and we tried our best to lead by example. Years would pass by, and we stayed together through all of the rough spots in life. We kept loving each other and staying committed to each other.

In 1993 we both accepted and dedicated our lives to living for God and to allow him to be first above all else, and we were so excited. We were enjoying our new life and spent much time learning about God and his ways. Years later, he accepted his call as pastor and he started his ministry in our home, which later moved to a storefront location for the next 3 years.

We later purchased our first church building and we both ministered as we were led by God. He was so excited and he said, "I can go to glory now because I feel like I've done the things God had for me to do, and I know that the Lord is with me." I didn't think anything of this statement at the time.

Our 25th wedding anniversary was quickly approaching and I was planning a big anniversary celebration. I wanted us to do a rehearsed couple's dance. He had just agreed to take dance lessons with me. He never had any rhythm, so this would take many lessons and practice. He often laughed and said he was probably one of the few pastors that God didn't give a singing voice or any rhythm, and this was so true. He had the gift of preaching and was very excited to do so, and he did it well, so I always told him to stay in his lane. I told him that he preached so well that God didn't want him to sing because he may never let us out of the church with singing and preaching.

God blessed our union and we were married without any separation for almost 25 years. Each time we ran into one of our classmates, they would be surprised that we were still married after all these years. They would ask if we were still together after all of these years. We smiled and said yes. We never understood why people were so amazed at us still being together since high school. We just thought that two people in love were supposed to be together forever as long as there weren't any true deal breakers. You see, in times of old, couples actually stayed together until death parted them as long as they remained in a safe and protected union.

We had problems and issues just like any couple does. The difference is that we stayed committed to one another and worked through them all. We were friends and in our early years of marriage, my dad gave us a title for our marriage that would carry us over the next 25 years. He looked at us and told us that he was reminded of a song when he saw us. That song title was; "Love conquers all" by Lionel Richie. Neither of us knew that this lined up with the word that teaches us that love really is the greatest gift of all.

We continued living our lives with love and the commitment we made to each other. I'm so thankful to share with the world how we had a good strong marriage for the duration of our time together. We were doing great. He was a pastor and I was a minister as well. One day our time together was up and little did I know that grief was soon to be my journey.

In our previous years, it was in my heart to write a book that I thought would be on marriage. I assumed it was for both of us to write it. One Saturday, as we finished lunch, I told him we needed to start writing the book, and his response was for me to start writing it. I thought this was his humor kicking in once again, but he had a serious look on his face, although I never knew what it was about. I never thought I would be writing this as my first book. I looked and asked him if he was going to help me write, and he gently said, "No, but I will be your inspiration." I didn't quite understand that, but for some reason, I accepted it.

Going back to previous years, Ken always teased our daughter and told her when it was time for her to get married, he was going to walk her down the aisles and perform the ceremony as well. She told him, "No, daddy, just walk me down the aisle. You can't do both." In March of 2005, he did just that. He not only walked her down the aisle, but he also performed the ceremony.

A few short years later, he officiated the ceremony for our son's wedding as well.

Life was going well for us. After all, we both tried to live according to God's word. We both were in ministry and the church was doing well. We had a good marriage; our kids were doing well and our home life was good. We followed God's plan.

CHAPTER TWO

THE PLANS

I was planning our 25th-year anniversary celebration. It was going to be a black and white ball. Only formal wear was to be worn. I had already designed my dress in my mind. A few months before this planning I had asked my husband if he would take some dance lessons so that we could do a dance for our guests during the celebration. The kids and I always teased him because he had no rhythm at all. I knew it would take months for the instructor to teach him how to do any type of two steps. He first said no, he wasn't going to do a dance. After months of me charming him and asking him again, he finally agreed to take the dance lessons with me.

I was so excited and I started to write down the plans. The place of the event was already chosen and it was going to be fabulous after all this was going to be our 25th year anniversary. I was planning for the best of everything. I had chosen the finest of linens and the tastiest foods and deserts. The room would be amazingly elegant. Everything was to be done with excellence.

I was preparing all of this in January because our anniversary was in December and I had already started saving money for the occasion. People were already chosen to help put this major event together. After all, how many couples do you know that get married the same year they graduated from high school at the age of 18 years old and remain married all these years without any domestic violence, separation, or any outside families.

We were so thankful to God for seeing us through all the obstacles we faced throughout our marriage. We knew that this was almost unheard of, but we also knew God had a plan for our lives. We were a growing ministry and we were enjoying the journey and the fruits of our labor.

I continued with the planning. I also had a surprise planned for him at this event. I had just spoken with a dance instructor and she had agreed to teach me an inspirational dance for this event. I wanted to surprise him with a special song along with a dance from me. This would be just a small token of my love for him.

Our daughter (Kenitra) was my confidant at the time, so I would tell her of all my plans because she would be the one helping me with this major event. Our son was never too good at keeping good secrets. He just couldn't stand it, and most of the time all you had to do was ask him what the other person was planning. Although he wouldn't straight out answer you if I started guessing, his face and his smile told the story. He would always say daddy got a good gift or surprise for you and with a little probing, I always knew. Ken would take advantage of this, so I had to stop telling Kenneth II (Mista) About my plans.

In the few years leading up to this, we began to take trips to places we hadn't been before and do some of the things we had never done before, such as taking a helicopter ride and going horseback riding. Our kids were grown and we were enjoying life. We were having so much fun.

We had finally learned how to vacation without taking the weight of the church with us. We were off on another trip that was very special because the church members had sent us on an all-expense-paid trip. We had nothing to do but to show up. Once we got to our destination, we were forbidden to pay for anything. Our breakfast lunch and dinner were already planned and paid for. They had even taken care of the tips in advance. Arrangements were made for us to have facials, manicures, pedicures, and full-body massages that would make you relax and fall asleep.

The next morning, we were off to the helicopter ride that would ride us over several cities.

After this trip, I started writing down my thoughts of how the anniversary ball would be and I was so excited. We had talked about our anniversary the entire time we were on this trip. Of course, I was planning to have the prettiest dress and shoes in the building. After all, I was the bride and it was our moment. Everything in our life seemed to be in order at this point and the planning was in full force.

Everything in our life seemed to have fallen into place and we were truly thankful to have each other. We were having the time of our life. I had no clue that something so heartbreaking was about to disrupt my life.

Jeremiah 29:11 (AMPC)

[11] For I know the thoughts and plans that I have for you, says the Lord, thoughts and plans for welfare and peace and not for evil, to give you hope in your final outcome.

CHAPTER THREE
JOURNALS FROM MY HEART

I began writing around 2:50pm on Monday 03/17/2008

I miss your brilliant smile, the smell of your cologne, and your natural scent.

I keep seeing you and imagining that I'm holding you and never letting you go. We had so many plans to do so many things and one day we ran out of time. I keep thinking in my head about how I was going to dance for you on our anniversary as a surprise, and although I didn't get a chance to do that dance for you, I remember dancing for you in the room for about two weeks before you left. I remember the big smile it brought across your handsome brown face. I love you.

Another long day

I keep thinking our dance ended too soon, but I'm reminded that I had you for 25 wonderful years of marriage and a total of 28 years in my life. Not only were we husband and wife but you were my friend. We shared everything even when the conversations hurt, we made it thru all the trials and storms and we knew that nothing would separate us. We knew death would have to part us because our love would remain forever.

April 2008

I'm trying with everything in me to continue to live a good life because I know you always wanted the very best for me. I see your smile every day, but it now brings tears to my eyes because I can't touch you. I'm going to continue to love you and have wonderful memories of you until we meet again.

Day Unknown

I can't even remember what day it is because they seem to be sooooo long now without you. As you know, I haven't been back to work since you left this earth. I never understood how a company could expect anyone who loses a spouse to come back in three days. Well, not me! Why didn't you fight to stay here with us?

May 2008

It's my birth month, but I'm definitely not up for celebrating. All I can feel is pain, sadness, and heartache. My heart feels like it's crumbling into pieces. With God being first as the head of my life, you were first here on earth."You made me feel secure. You will forever be in my heart. I will write to you again very soon. I Love You

June 2008

It's class reunion time and I don't plan to go because it's too hard without you. I can't even bring myself to be a part of the committee this time because it hurt too much. Too many memories. You know we always won the award for being married the longest, but this time it will be different without you. Why did you leave me like this? Nothing will ever be the same. I miss you so much!!!!

I think it's Thursday 9:41am

I woke up again with you on my mind and heart. I picked up the pillow with your picture on it and read it once again. Your radiant smile took my breath away. It almost seems like you were posing just for me. I took it as a sign to try and live a good life because you tried to give me the best life possible within your means. I decided if I'm going to win over my grief, I have to win big because to barely cope just means I'm existing and not living life to the fullest.

2:13am I can't sleep

I kept hearing your words when I asked if you were going to help me write our book, and your reply was, "I'm going to be your inspiration". Now I fully understand what that means.

You have always been my inspiration and always wanted the best for me. Now I will try my best from this moment on living life to the fullest. Meaning I will continue to put God first and I will explore the world.

When I say I must win big, here is what I mean; I must not put off until tomorrow things I can do today. I will write as many books as I can, I will travel as much as I can, and I will inspire and motivate others as hard as I can. I will continue to dream big and expect great things. Most of all, always putting God first was the most important thing we had in common.

With every passing day, I asked God to reverse this life-changing event and bring you back to me. I know we loved each other unconditionally. One day I will have to release you in order to free myself from this torture that I feel.

You… my love will always be a part of my life.

I LOVE YOU

July 2008

It's about 4:28 pm and my day started off okay, but by now I'm missing every part of you, followed by a gush of anger. I keep saying to myself how silly it is to be mad at the one you love because you feel like he left you here hurting. But through it all, I still LOVE YOU.

Monday 06/09/2008

Happy Birthday my love. This seems to be all I can get out on this day. This hurts and brings fond memories at the same time. You always tried to find out what your gift would be ahead of time by any means necessary. Our kids know exactly what I mean. Ken, we MISS you so much.

06/24/08

It's been a few weeks since I wrote to you, but I still think about you every single day and I'm still imagining what the two of us would be doing or how I would be dressing to take your breath away.

I now have some okay days, but never do I forget the Love we shared. I still tell the Lord almost every day that he could still bring you back to earth to be with us, but I know you wouldn't want to come back here to the cares of this world.

I'm having second thoughts about leading the ministry because it all seems overwhelming sometimes. I also know that I wasn't called to Pastor. I always told you and the congregation that yes, I would preach in church, but more of my ministry was outside of the four walls of the building. I'm praying for direction from the Lord.

PS: I love you

07/06/08

I finally started going back to my parent's house on Sundays. For the first two months, it was too hard, mainly because you were no longer with me. Besides, all of my family looked forward to you walking through the door since you were the life of the party and the family comedian.

When I manage to get the strength to go, I can never stay long because it's so hard seeing the pain of losing you on everyone's face because they're missing you, and hurting for me at the same time.

07/15/2008

Hello handsome. Just wanted to give you a progress report. I finally started pushing through and going places without leaving out crying or cutting my visit short. I realized that I had to push through and that it was okay to have conversations about you even if we all cried together. I realized this was healthy for me. I also realized that when I'm having a fairly good day to not allow others' grief to camp out with me. I would simply tell them I'm having a strong day, and they understood.

October 2008

I finally sat down from the ministry to start my healing journey. I'm following the doctor's instructions and mainly Gods leading. He put on my heart to visit another church while I was healing so I wouldn't be pulled on by the members because I had to go through my own journey of allowing him to heal me. My body was so sick and our doctor said I was grieving really hard that it was making my body physically ill.

. . .

Throughout the early part of 2009

I continued journaling as I was becoming stronger every day because I truly learned how to transfer my burdens to the Lord. The scripture didn't just sound good to quote, but it became alive in my life. Yes, the word became ALIVE and active in my life. I was experiencing the truth of God's word. His strength was truly made perfect in my weakness. When I thought I couldn't go on, God proved that I could and I did.

Years 2009-present

This was just the beginning of my journaling. I did it on a regular basis as it was very therapeutic for me.

Throughout the years after the death of my spouse, I motivated, helped, and coached many through grief in many areas of life, from the death of a loved one, marriage crisis, divorce, and a host of other losses. The urgency to turn my journey of recovery into this book is why you're reading it today.

I started this book years ago, but today my prayer is that it will motivate and inspire others to live and not die and to become all that God desires for us to become. This is how I continually pay it forward to help others along the way.

CHAPTER FOUR
WITHOUT WARNING

Mmy husband had hurt his back many years ago and his doctor was concerned with the pain because it was going from his back and all the way down his legs and feet. The doctor arranged an overnight hospital stay for testing only. We were to check-in at noon on Monday morning. The doctor said since he wanted several tests done, such as CT scans and MRI this would be the quickest way to get it done and have results instantly.

All-day Monday things seem to be smooth sailing. We talked and watched TV since I was staying overnight with him. The next morning, I noticed my husband was in more pain and talking less. I asked any medical staff that came in the room what time they would be taking him to test but never got a clear answer.

I noticed he was struggling a little with his breathing, so I told the nurses and any staff that would listen that something was wrong because I was hearing a mist on the inside of him. It seemed as if no one was listening to me until one nurse listened and said she would get the doctor. By this time, they finally came to get him for testing.

Evening came and my daughter walked into the room with our two angels, at least that's what I called them. They were our nieces (Davione & Daja) who at that time lived with us. We loved them as if they were our own. He smiled at them while trying to muster up the strength to talk and play with them. Of course, they got in the hospital bed with him; they didn't care that it wasn't enough room. When it was time for them to leave, he kissed them and told them he loved them.

I began to pick up around the room because I brought books and magazines to read to pass the time during what I thought would be an overnight stay.

Tuesday morning came and still no tests had been done. Around 1:00 pm they came to get him for his tests. About 1.5 hours had passed and he was being wheeled back into the room. My back was turned to the young man who transported him back to the room. He begins to call my name and asks, "Is Mr. Middleton normally this hard to wake up?"

As I turned around and saw my husband's face, I knew something was terribly wrong. He looked lifeless. I rushed over and touched him. He wasn't breathing and was cold to the touch. I yelled at the transporter, telling him to get help because he wasn't breathing. I could clearly tell this young man was in shock, so I had to yell for help while pressing the button to get help. The medical staff rushed in, said code blue and began the process of resuscitation. They told me to step outside of the room, but I told them I was staying and wouldn't get in their way. This wasn't a pretty sight, but they were able to revive him. They then decided to put him on oxygen.

Entering the room was a tall salt and peppered hair doctor who identified himself as the pulmonologist. I knew this wasn't a good sign. He asked me to explain what I was hearing in Ken's breathing. The best way I could describe it was as a misting sound as if there was something draining in his throat. I will never forget the look on the doctor's face when he said, "I hope that you're wrong because this could mean he is aspirating." He said it could be his own saliva, the contents of stomach acids, or a type of Pneumonia.

As the day went on, it was silent. Although he walked into the hospital talking, this was no longer the case. He could only listen to my voice at this point. I kept praying and trying to reassure him that everything would be alright, and he would just shake his head in agreement. After hours of this, the nodding of the head turned into a peculiar look as if he was trying to communicate something to me.

As hours passed, I would have to look at him and take deep breaths so he could do the same because his oxygen levels kept dropping lower than it should have. I began to ask them how I would know when the breathing monitor was too low so that I could alert them if necessary. They told me what number to look for. So, the rest of the day when the number would drop low, I would touch him and say breathe with me, as I would take a few deep breaths for him to follow.

This went on for hours until the medical staff noticed the oxygen wasn't helping and decided to intubate him. I realized at this moment he was being put on life support. My world as I knew it was swiftly changing without notice. They decided he needed to be put into the Critical Care Unit. So, I had to leave the hospital because there was no space to stay in that type of room with him. I left the hospital around midnight and returned around 8:00 am the next morning.

During the next several hours my husband showed no signs of life because he couldn't talk back to me. I continued to speak life over him. I continued believing in faith for a miracle. I was speaking into his ear while touching his heart, reciting healing scriptures, and telling him how much I loved him. I told him that he needed to fight and come back to us all.

It was Wednesday, March 12th, 2008, and the specialist walked into the room and informed me that Ken was the sickest patient in CCU, but he couldn't give me a specific reason why this was the case. I raised my voice and told him that he wasn't this sick coming into this hospital. At least, I didn't think so.

Although still in disbelief, I realized I needed to inform our daughter and son of their dad's status.

During this short period of time making these two phone calls, he coded once again. The doctor and medical staff told me to step out of the room once again. For the second time, I had to tell them in a nice voice that I was staying in the room and that I would remain out of their way. Only this time I knew the outcome would be different because this was the second time using the defibrillator to try and bring him back.

While standing against the wall praying and holding on to my faith and hope, my legs began to give out and I was slowly going down. A nurse saw me and held me up as she lovingly walked me right outside of the room to a chair.

My son appeared at the hospital saying he just couldn't work that day because he knew something was wrong. Next, one of Ken's sisters (Valerie) walked up and she said the same thing. I then proceeded to call our daughter to inform her that she needed to get to the hospital asap.

By noon on that Wednesday morning, the doctor was walking toward us. It looked like a scene on television with the doctor coming my way. As he got closer, he put his head down. Although I saw him, I was saying to myself, "he's going to tell me my husband wasn't doing well, but I will just continue praying and believing that he will be okay." The doctor then said, "I did everything I could, but he's gone. I sat in my chair for what seemed to be ten minutes in disbelief without any response. I felt totally blind-sided.

This scene with the doctor walking toward me, shaking his head and looking very disappointed, was something I saw on television many times. This time the scene was real and it was happening to me.

I realized the doctor wasn't changing his mind, so it finally soaked in that my husband was gone without any warning. I had to get up because I felt the need to walk. When I tried to walk, I fell down to the floor in utter despair and disbelief. My first words were, "God, what are you doing, and why did you allow this to happen?" I was telling God that he knew we were in ministry and tried to live according to his will.

After the initial shock my next sentence to the Lord would be, "Lord, I believe, but now you will have to help my unbelief because I can't believe you allowed this to happen." At his point, my heart was broken. I can't describe the pain that I felt. It's like no other pain I've ever had in my life.

Sometimes storms come without warning us that it's headed our way. I wasn't the first to go through it and I knew I wouldn't be the last. Just know that you can get through it. I know it was God carrying me through this because I had no power, energy, or ability to get through this without crying out to him for my strength

Philippians 4:13(AMPC) I have strength for all things in Christ Who empowers me [I am ready for anything and equal to anything through Him Who [a]infuses inner strength into me; I am [b]self-sufficient in Christ's sufficiency].

CHAPTER FIVE

DENIAL

Although I dropped to my knees at the hospital in utter despair, a few days had passed by and it was time to plan for the burial. By this time, I jumped into a total working mode to give him what's called a proper burial. Although I was preparing for the service, it was still very surreal. I just knew the service had to be done right and I wanted to get it over with. Even though this was the planning stage, I was still in denial. Every time the phone would ring, I would run to it in hopes that it would be the hospital saying they made a mistake and my husband was alive even though I saw his lifeless body. It still seemed to be a bad dream and I hoped I would soon wake up from it. During this time, I continued to ask God to let this be a horrible nightmare that would end.

I continued with my imagined story of the doctors calling me, and it would have gone something like this; *Hello Lisa, this is Dr. _____. I called to apologize. We made a terrible mistake. We realized we had a John Doe here in the hospital that has been in a coma for a while. The person we pronounced dead wasn't your husband but someone that looked identical to him. Your husband is out of the coma and you can come and see him now.*

This was weeks after the burial, and this was still my created scenario that I rehearsed in my mind daily. After each imaginary phone call from the hospital, I imagined myself grabbing my keys and running out of the door. Now I never told anyone else of my imaginary conversations with the doctor because, in my mind, I had to go and see him first. Then I would call our kids and his siblings and tell them to meet me at the hospital and just let them see for themselves. Well, that day never happened and months had passed and I was still in disbelief.

During this time of grieving, there was no way I could just go right back to work, so I took a few months off from work. I just knew I couldn't fully concentrate on doing any type of work at this point in my life. I was grieving really hard most of the time. After finishing up all the household business, the house was now super quiet. I knew it was time to return to work because the walls seemed to be closing in on me and I began to hate being at our house. You see, this was our home and he was no longer there, so I went back to work.

Each day at the end of my shift my co-worker would smile at me because he noticed when my husband was living. I would always freshen up my perfume so I could go home smelling nice. This habit never changed because somewhere in the back of my mind, I thought I would still see the miracle of him being home when I got there, or at least this is what I had hoped.

On the drive home each day, once I got off of the main highway to get to my house, it was approximately four miles from the exit to my house. As soon as I would exit, I would smile and start to tell myself 'I'm going home to give my husband a kiss because the highlight of my day was seeing his face after dealing with everything at work'. Well, this part didn't change after he died. I would get off of the highway and say I'm going to give my husband … I had to realize and tell myself he was no longer there and this always led to tears.

The second phase of my denial came months later when I realized there was one part of the burial that I didn't complete. Although the funeral had been over for months now, I did everything that I was supposed to do except order his headstone because, in my mind, this would mean that I was giving up on what I daydreamed about for so long. At one point, I forgot about it, I truly think I was trying to avoid it because this would mean finality.

Deny what I see? Oh no, not me
I was trying to claim the victory.
I wouldn't accept what was right in my face
That my husband was gone from this wicked place.
Away from this earth of sorrow and pain
I knew he wouldn't choose to come here again.
To sin, sickness, and sorrow all through the land,
Who on earth would choose this type of pain?
Denial won't change anyone's story or plight
It was time to open up and accept my new life.
Lisa T

CHAPTER SIX

HELP I'M STILL HURTING

I was always private about my personal business and I didn't talk much about my personal life with friends or family. One had to be extremely close to me for me to share my personal business with them. However, my insides were screaming for someone to help me. Can't you see that my heart is broken"?

My belief is that everyone at some point in life will need the love and support of others to help them through a crisis or major life event. Don't let your status, pride, or anything else stop you from being honest about needing support. There's a saying that only the strong survive and that is so true, but only if you're strong enough to know you need the support of others at times.

For far too long we had been led to believe that we shouldn't trust or be vulnerable to others because it makes us look like we're weak or that others will talk about us. On one hand, there are the church folks who that believe when you show signs of distress, you don't have any faith, but this is a lie straight from the devil.

The bible tells us to get wisdom because it's the principal thing. You see, my deceased husband and I were in ministry together, so we were the leaders. I'm so thankful that I had wisdom enough to know that this pain was too hard for me to handle alone and that I needed help. I didn't care what the church folks or others around me would think; I just knew I needed help even with having faith.

I had to first admit that I was hurting and needed their support. Yes, I have been a leader most of my life and people have always called on me for help and encouragement. For me, it wasn't so much about how people saw me. I just wasn't used to my new dynamics. I was the motivator, encourager, and the helper. Sometimes when you have a tender heart for helping others, it's hard to accept it for yourself. Wisdom told me that if I was a good leader, then those close to me would know how to take the reign and lead when necessary. I have always said if you're a great leader, then you will help others around you to be great leaders as well. Well, it paid off. I started letting my circle know if I needed company, or if I just needed time to cry without being rescued. I knew that I had to go through my process.- During this time of pain my true friends took charge, my family was amazing and my daughter became the leader that I taught her to be even through her pain. This was such a blessing to me to have their support and love. When I allowed them to help me in my weakness, their support gave me the strength I needed to go on. Some days I would actually initiate the call to tell them I needed some company. Although this wasn't what I would normally do, I knew I couldn't do it alone.

Months passed and everyone seemed to be shying away from me because they also felt the loss and didn't know what to say. They didn't want to show their pain in front of me because they thought it would make things worse. Of course, their pain wasn't of the same magnitude as mine, but they still felt the pain of this enormous loss. I then realized we didn't have to hide from each other because of being emotional, but we could talk and cry together.

One agreement that I had to have was that everyone in my circle would still treat me the same. This is what I meant; if we were humorous with each other before this time of loss, let's not stop now. Don't add to it or try to downplay what happened, but don't stop making me laugh. Pity wasn't going to help me move forward in the healing process. This was an unfamiliar heartache like nothing I had ever felt before. It felt like I had open heart surgery without anesthesia.

One of the first things I had to admit was that this was a major life event unlike any other. Many times, when my phone would ring, even if it was my best girlfriend, I would talk for a few minutes and then just admit to her that this was a rough day. Doing this let them know that I needed them, so the next thing I knew, one of them would show up at my doorstep, even if it was just to sit with me quietly.

This was different for me because it was my natural gift from God to be a motivator, encourager, and minister. Now I was the one needing all of this. Don't let your pride or status stop you from reaching out. Don't worry that people are used to seeing you as the strong one, but now it seems you are weak. Yes, indeed, I was now the weaker one needing to be encouraged and in need of much prayer. Just acknowledging that I was weak during this time is what made me strong enough to seek help. By doing this, my amazing sisters took charge on many occasions and sometimes, late on Friday nights, they would call everyone, including some other close family and friends, to join us. We would all meet at IHOP for a late-night breakfast. This worked wonders for me. Although many of the times I didn't have an appetite, the laughter and the fellowship meant the world to me.

Sometimes we take it for granted that people know what we need, but that's not always true. I remember when one of my best friend's moms had passed away. Although I was there for the funeral services, I really didn't have a clue what she needed from me. Now going through this process, I understand better how to support people and even how to give them some space at the same time.

When I returned to work after many months, I was still in so much pain, but I knew that I needed to start my new reality. I needed to even tell my close co-workers as well as my manager how I needed their help. It would be days when I was on the phone with a customer and out of seemingly nowhere, the grief would hit me. I would then email my manager and tell her I was leaving for the day. This happened a few times and they always worked with me. I knew that I couldn't just keep running off every time I had a meltdown. There was no reason to be ashamed to cry or have a meltdown.

I was having the natural response to grief. The next time I was on the phone with a client and had a moment of grief and began to cry, I would simply ask the person to hold on. I then summoned one of my team members, mainly (Rhonda Broadnax) with tears rolling down my face to finish the call for me.

She always came through for me when this happened at work. I walked away from my desk and went to the sitting area in the restroom and cried out to God for his help and strength, and then I returned to my desk to complete my work.

My tears weren't a sign of weakness. Not allowing myself to accept help would have led to a lifetime of depression and I refused to camp out there. I had a saying if someone came around me when I had good days and they wanted to be sad or feel sorry for me, I would say, "I'm not camping out there todayThis actually helped me so much.

There were moments when I was home alone and I realized that it was okay for me to scream to the top of my lungs in agony. This was my way of releasing what I was feeling.

After you're crying is over, then get up and do something positive. Don't let life beat you up. Cry out, scream loud, and fall to the floor if you must but keep fighting to move past the hurt and pain that can lead you to a never-ending pit.

Although I was hurting, I decided that the world still needed me in it. My voice needed to be heard around the world to encourage and lift someone else up through this time in their life. I know that if people understood what I've been through and made it then they would be encouraged not to let anything in life stop them from reaching their purpose.

Still Hurting

Help, I'm still hurting. Why didn't everyone see?
How in the world could I get the victory?
The pain was so deep and embedded in my heart
How could my loved one so soon depart?
Only God has the answers and knows what is best
I just want to make sure that I passed this test
The measure of my faith was tested and tried
Throughout this time on God, I still relied
There was nothing I could do but lift up my hands
Somehow, I still knew that God still had a master plan

Lisa

CHAPTER SEVEN
MIDNIGHT HOUR

Sleep had left my body for months. I was still in a haze and wondering what was happening to my life. I laid down to rest and did everything I could think of to try and get some sleep. Nothing seemed to be working.

The first few nights when I was awakened in the middle of the night, I would just lay there wondering how I got to this place. The nights afterward I would lay there and pray just a little. Days kept passing by and I realized this is getting ready to be a regular awakening for a while. So, I finally gave in and said I'm not gone, just lay here. Music was a healing agent for me, so I would listen as I wrote and waited for God to speak to my heart.

It was in the midnight hours that I could really hear the words because of the busyness of the day. This episode in my life was unplanned and I had no choice or say in the matter. Death just seemed to have crept into my life without me being prepared.

The midnight hour seemed to be dark and everything that was once familiar was gone. God had allowed some things and some people to be moved away from my surroundings at this point in my journey. I didn't understand what he was doing or why. I just knew he was at work somehow in my life. Although the pain in my heart felt like I was hurting beyond reason, I knew for sure that God didn't allow these circumstances to harm or overtake me.

In life, we all will have some kind of midnight experience, whether it is a death of a loved one, a divorce, or some other type of loss. They all come with some of the same emotions and pain. Your midnight hour could mean a loss in many different areas of your life, such as death, loss of employment, house, cars, marriage, and a host of other losses. It may sometimes feel that you're invisible.

The friend you thought would always be in your life now has a new circle of friends. Your heart is very sad, but you finally come to the realization that you're in a different season in your life, and in order to win, you must embrace your new season even if it seems like you're in a wilderness.

Begin to go with the flow in your midnight hour and realize almost everything around you is changing and something is happening in your atmosphere. You may not be able to force a smile out. My question to God at this time went something like this; God, what are you doing, and how am I supposed to be at this time in my new reality? I just sat there in silence, feeling hopeless and waiting for a magical answer to solve my current problem. Then I remembered change is inevitable! As long as we live here on this earth, there will always be change.

Quickly I learned to flow in the midst of darkness and I allowed God to do his work in my life. This is the time when he was giving me an increase in my very soul because I availed myself. That was the only way I could go on by allowing God's almighty power to rise up in me and to show himself strong and mighty through me, even with the tears. My praise on the inside was rising up again. It now felt like I would burst if I didn't let it out.

My sleepless nights started because of the stress of losing my husband along with the grief and pain that I was in. At the same time, a bigger purpose was trying to burst out. It's the season that was already chosen without my vote. I started going with the flow and watched God transform my new normal.

Even though I lay on the floor and cried in agony, yelled, screamed, and cried some more while telling God this was too hard to deal with, it still didn't change the reality and it certainly didn't bring my husband back. It was then I realized that no matter how much I yelled, screamed, or cried, it didn't change the season I was in.

It's now time to stop asking why did this happen to me and decide to live life to the fullest because we don't know when our time will be up. I decided while I'mhere, I didn't just want to exist because that's worse than a physical death. Instead, I wanted to live life with a purpose to fulfill.

In this life sometimes everyone needs a good cry, but then you have to get up and live again

It's time to come out of the midnight hour and accept your change. After all, there's nothing you can do to turn things

around. Once you embrace the season you're in, then you're
ready to move forward.

This is the season God wants to whisper his mysteries and
secrets into our hearts. We need to quiet ourselves wait on him
and rest in his presence. Be still and just listen to your heart.
Allow yourself to be drawn closer to him. Stop trying to figure
everything out and go with the flow. Only in his presence can
the answer be received. Our minds require some type of order
to function properly. Our days are so busy we can't decipher
much. That's why he chooses these midnight hours to bring
about revelation and give us glimpses of his purpose for us.

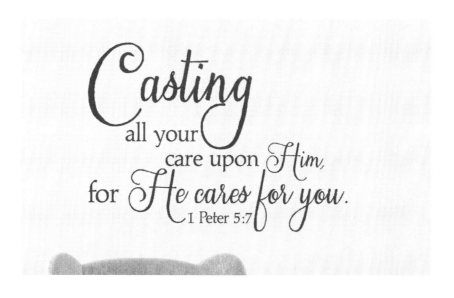

CHAPTER EIGHT

HELP MY UNBELIEF

In the midst of me writing this book, I had an appointment with my retina specialist on a Thursday morning. I had been in prayer all morning long. My doctor told me I had blood vessels that were bleeding in the back of my eye, which could result in vision loss. My vision was already distorted at this point. I had to make a decision in the fifteen minutes that I was waiting for the test results to reveal if his thoughts were correct. He came back with the report and it was what he suspected. My thoughts were racing in my head as to whether or not to try this new procedure. I had to remember God uses many different ways of healing us, so I decided to have the procedure right there in the office.

While I was sitting and waiting for the procedure, my thoughts were: Okay, God, haven't I been through enough? After all, I'm still grieving the loss of my husband. Isn't that enough?

On another day, I received a phone call from one of my doctors saying I needed to see the specialists because it seemed that I had developed stomach ulcers which could quickly turn to cancer. Wow!!! I began to wonder if I had done something wrong to bring all of this into my life. I had to simply realize along with grieving comes stress which is natural, but you have to learn how to release and deal with stress because it will deal with you and manifest itself in your body if you don't

The thought came to me that I must have something awesome to offer the world. I then heard the words, "just believe". After all, I still had my sound mind through all of this and I wasn't in a state of depression. Even though there were moments of this during this time. I was still walking out my God-given purpose. So, I laughed and said to the enemy aren't you tired of losing? I didn't lose my mind and now this. I kept saying to myself that I was healed already through the power of God. At this moment, I knew that I would be completely whole and healed, and I would continue to listen to God's leading. I knew there were greater blessings awaiting me if I just held on.

All of this was going on while I was releasing things in my old life and awaiting God's direction for my new life to begin. The old was being finalized and everything around me seemed to be new and fresh and I thanked him through the pain. Even at a time like this, I was in amazement at where God had me in my thoughts and in my new reality. All I thought of at this point was that God had moved me forward through such a horrific time when I thought I couldn't get through it. At this point, I said Lord, I still believe you, but please help any unbelief that I may have. I had to just believe God for continually healing me.

This was a time when I was questioning God like never before. I was still in disbelief of how in the blink of an eye, my life seemed to have turned upside down.

Don't let anyone make you feel guilty for asking God to make himself known to you during times like this because it's just a natural response to something so painful. Just remember, sometimes your answers won't come as you think they should. The first response may be to just believe. I remember in the bible there was a man that told God I believe but helps my unbelief. I could now relate to this man because all these years prior to the death of my spouse, I believed and trusted God, but this was like no other experience I had been through, so I needed some help.

Religious folks will make you think you're crazy for feeling this way or that you can pray anything away. Unless you're in a particular situation yourself, then you really don't know how you will feel. It's easy for people on the outside looking in to say this or that, but they don't have a clue. That's why a personal relationship instead of being religious is of the utmost importance.

I knew I was right on the verge of a major breakthrough. I knew without a doubt God had blessings far above my imagination waiting for me. So, I released everything in my life to God because I knew he could carry my burdens much better than I could. That was too much weight for me to handle alone.

I decided to release all of my feelings to God and the counselor. Oops, did I say the bad word, counselor?

Some things will happen in this life that we aren't prepared for and we need the help of others. After all, God is the one who gifted people to have the expertise to help us through times like this as long as we're still trusting and following his guidance. We get so caught up in the cultural belief of not going to see a counselor.

In me releasing my thoughts and telling God, I couldn't get through this without his help. He did help me by leading me to a counselor. The counselor decided after a few short visits that I was just fine and going through the normal process of grieving. I'm so glad I went because I didn't know if the feelings I was having were normal.

She gave me strategies and exercises that helped me sleep a little better. All of this without any medicine. So, don't be afraid to seek help while trusting God.

In saying just believe we have to be open to how God wants to help us and not get caught up in what others think. My counselor looked at me, smiled, and said, "You will be just fine and I have no doubt that you will get through this, but you will also help others."

I decided to believe in living life on purpose because someone else is depressed, desperate, and without hope. I may be the person to help them through it. I knew God was still working through me in the midst of my grieving. When family members and friends would come around, I could feel their pain and it was therapy for me to comfort and encourage them also.

We have to sit back and still trust and believe even when life seems to give us some unexpected blows. We can keep moving forward and make the most of the precious time we have here on earth.

Mark 9:24 (KJV)
And straightway the father of the child cried out, and said with tears, Lord, I believe; help thou mine unbelief.

Mark 9:24 (AMPC)

[24] At once the father of the boy gave [an [a]eager, [b]piercing, inarticulate] cry *with tears*, and he said, Lord, I believe! [Constantly] help my [c]weakness of faith!

CHAPTER NINE

THE UNKNOWN

Many years ago, while typing some of my thoughts, I was wondering what was going on at this stage of my life. At times it seemed like I was in a season of overflow and the next minute, life was frozen in time with no excitement.

God seemed to be blessing mightily, then all of a sudden, it seemed like everything around me was numb and silent. I asked the Lord what was going on because, in my head, I had already fought through many obstacles over the years. I didn't feel like fighting anymore.

The older generation used to sing a song that said, " I don't feel no ways tired." I agree with the latter part of the song that says, "I don't believe he brought me this far to leave me." But I was definitely tired physically and emotionally during this particular journey. If others would be honest, they get tired too. The blessing isn't whether you get tired or not. The blessing is that you keep going. Even when the unknown occurs, you have to decide to keep pushing, praying, and prevailing. Knowing there is a prize awaiting you.

At this point, all I could say is, "God, you know I love you. Lord, you know I believe; I just need your mighty hand to take me through this. The victory is being honest before the Lord and allowing him to help you through this mysterious time."

God already knows all of your thoughts, so you might as well come before him naked. When it seems like you don't know what's going on around you, this is the time God wants us to just trust and believe him.

During this time of the unknown God is always working in the spirit realm. He uses this process to make us stronger and more determined to believe him through the rough spots. Even though we can't see what's going on, he wants us to see ourselves as he sees us. We must see the victory before it comes. There's a song that says Lord help me believe I am what you see. Ask the Lord to help you to see what he sees.

He knows our ending from the very beginning. He didn't bring you this far to leave you. The only thoughts God has for you and meare thoughts of good and not evil. He has purposed for us to win. That was the whole point of the cross so that nothing can separate us from him.

Romans 8:35-39 KJV

Who shall separate us from the love of Christ? Shall tribulation, or distress, or persecution, or famine, or nakedness, or peril, or sword? As it is written, for thy sake, we are killed all the day long; we are accounted as sheep for the slaughter. Nay, in all these things, we are more than conquerors through him that loved us. For I am persuaded that neither death, nor life, nor angels, nor principalities, nor powers, nor things present, nor things to come, nor height, nor depth, nor any other creature, shall be able to separate us from the love of God, which is in Christ Jesus our Lord.

CHAPTER TEN

LETTING GO

One day I got a phone call from our daughter saying, "Mom, it's time to order daddy's headstone because it's been months now." I told her I knew but I didn't know if I was ready. Well, the funeral home called me to inquire about his headstone as well. This was on a Monday morning. I told them just give me until tomorrow. In the meantime, I began to pray and tell God exactly how I felt. By this time, I knew I needed to close this chapter because this was unhealthy and the stress on my body was taking its toll on my health.

I tried to choose it during the time I was making funeral arrangements, but it was so overwhelming. I had done all that I could do at that moment without totally breaking down. He told me I could choose it after the homegoing services. Yet it had been months and I still hadn't dealt with that part. I guess in my head, that would be the finale.

A few of the family members didn't understand why I hadn't put his headstone on his burial site. Although I didn't owe anyone an explanation, the only thing I would tell them is they couldn't possibly understand if they hadn't gone through it. People will always talk and speak about things they don't understand. I was even guilty of doing the same thing before this tragedy happened in my life. I now know that unless you've been through it, you don't have a clue as to how you will feel or how you will handle things.

The rest of the day seemed to be the longest day of my life, knowing that I would have to finally deal with this. I spent the rest of the day just praying to ask God to prepare my heart for this because I didn't know if I was ready to let go.

I knew I would have to do this alone. I shut myself off for the rest of Monday, trying to prepare for what I thought would be too hard to bear. I was reading and praying. Many complained and murmured about him not having a marker, but I didn't allow that to rush me to do something that only God could prepare me for.

It wasn't that I was trying to go without doing this part, but after the funeral, I guess they forgot to remind me until some time had passed. I would think about it from time to time, but mostly I was grieving from my broken heart.

Whatever you do, stop saying what you would do and that if it were you, you would handle things differently. The truth is you don't know. Trust me, you don't have a clue what you do until that day or situation comes. The night came and I couldn't sleep.

I was once again waking up every few hours with anxiety about the next day. Still praying through the night and saying, "God, you promised not to put more on me than I could bear, so I need you to see me through this horrific time.

I told God I would need his help because there was no way I could do this final piece, but at the same time, I knew it had to be done. Just as I prayed about it God had a way out for me. During my time of grief the one thing that never changed in my life was the nurturing nature that God gave me.

My baby sister (Yolanda) would call me saying how much she missed her brother-in-law. The two of them were very close because he always made her see life in a positive way. Ken was close to everyone in my family, but she thought he could fix any situation. Anytime this happened, I would begin to encourage and minister to her until I thought she felt better. This was always good therapy for me when I helped someone else feel better. Well, I never knew what was ahead of me.

The next morning finally got here. I got dressed and I prayed from the house to the funeral home. I continued to ask God for strength. I didn't ask anyone to go with me because when it's time to really let go, that's a job for you and God alone. No one else could help me or do it for me. I knew I had to decide to let go because that would be the beginning of the healing process.

Tuesday morning came just as I knew it would and I headed to the funeral home to choose and pay for his headstone. Money was never the issue. The issue was the finality of it all and I just wasn't ready to accept the fact that he wasn't coming back in the way I wanted him to.

I finally realized it was time to let go and deal with the life I was now living, the life of being by myself. I was still nervous as I walked into the funeral home. I stopped and glanced at the spot where my husband's body once was. The director came out and took me into his office to choose the marker, but something was different about him. He sat the pamphlet in front of me to choose the headstone but as I looked up, his face told me he was in so much pain.

While planning for funeral services, the funeral director and I had an instant spiritual connection. While planning and even speaking on the phone during that time, we would always end up talking about God and sharing. I was totally comfortable with him, so I knew if he called me, it was time.

I began to ask him where his beautiful wife was and he began to sob and tell me that she no longer wanted to be married and she wanted a divorce. I instantly went into my nurturing ministering mode. I put the pamphlet aside and grabbed both his hands and began to pray for him. I began to speak the word of God over his life, and I asked the Lord to heal him of his pain. We started talking and ministering to one another.

After that part was over, I looked at the pamphlet and was able to quickly pick out the headstone that I liked, but something was now different about me. I realized in my being so nervous and afraid to finalize this part of my life. God was healing me while I was helping someone else through their time of grief.

Once again, I realized life was not about me, and God didn't allow this event to happen just to hurt me. When God allows a life event to happen, he will use it to birth something in you related to his purpose for you. Sometimes we have life-changing events that hurt beyond words and we don't understand why, but we have to choose to move forward and not let it kill us. Although it may not kill us physically, if we don't decide to live again and move forward, we will only be breathing and existing without a real purpose in life.

This time I left with a smile because I was amazed at how God worked things out so that it wouldn't be too hard for me and at the same time, I would be helping someone else. God had allowed me to not focus on my pain. It was then that I realized once again that God was glorified in that very moment and that I was put here for a bigger purpose than even I could even imagine.

As I walked out, I looked up and saw the sun shining and I immediately had a new outlook on life and I decided God still needed to use me here on earth. He would take something that seemed too hard for me to do and turn it around and have me encourage and motivate someone else who was going through a life crisis. This let me know that I had to live again because somebody needed me to encourage, motivate and inspire them to live again instead of just existing.

I started to remember the day my husband passed away. I fell to the ground at the news from the doctor. I began to cry out in so much pain, but in the midst of my crying out, I asked God to make me better and not bitter. I knew instantly that what I was going through, no earthly creature would be able to help me with this. This was a job for the Lord and me, but I had to choose participate in my recovery.

You can choose to stay in the past, but the pain will remain the same in this state. This leads to a life of depression and hope-lessness. Or you can choose to live again and help someone else through their pain. I realized there were so many people who went years and years and never moved past their life-changing moment or event, but they remained stuck in time. This led to them being stagnant and not being able to make the turn in life.

You may still be in denial at this point but just know God wants you to live again, but this time with a purpose. Someone else loves you and needs you. If you feel as if your pain is unbearable, I agree with you. It is unbearable when you try to go through it alone. With God, all things are possible. Remember, God also places people and new opportunities in our life to help us through this time of pain. Life events will happen to all of us, but it doesn't have to stop us from living a meaningful life.

At the time I was writing these journals, there was still a great pain in my heart. I knew there was more that God wanted me to do. This meant I couldn't just exist, but I had to be INTENTIONAL about living and moving forward. Life will often reroute your journey and thrust us into a new direction. Don't fight it; EMBRACE it.

Denial didn't bring him back, so I had to find a way to embrace the new chapters of my life. I came to the realization that the pain didn't kill me, so I must be stronger. I could have decided to take a vacation from life and live in a depressed state or I could begin to see how I wanted my new life to play out.

The emotions of Blame, Shame nor Regret won't bring them back, nor will these emotions help the healing process. Don't allow the devil to keep you in the bondage of grief by blaming yourself. Forgive yourself and forgive the deceased, ex-spouse, or whatever and whoever you need to and move forward. None of these will bring them back.

Let Go

Letting go isn't easy nor is it light
But with God's help, we can win every fight
The glory, the victory, the power that is near
Will all play out if we don't camp out in fear
He does it much better than we can ever see
Because he formed us, we already have the victory
Whether on this side or the other you see
We have to lean into his power to truly be free
Lisa T

CHAPTER ELEVEN
MY DEFINING MOMENT

It was a beautiful sunny day. A nice day to have lunch on the beach and do a little shopping. Many times, my sisters would call and say hey, let's have a sister's day and do lunch and go shopping but this Saturday, I didn't hear from anyone. Normally when we do this, of course, our mother was always included in these sister days.

It was early in the morning and I decided to run a few errands and then make the phone call to see if I could treat someone to lunch and even a little shopping. Normally my daughter and my daughter-in-law would jump to the occasion of helping me spend my money on them, of course, but both had other plans this day.

This day was like no other day. I had friends in the past that was single and sometimes they would express to me how they would get lonely sometimes and how they wanted to be married so they wouldn't be lonely. I often explained to them that unless they begin to understand who they are and find some wholeness within themselves, then marriage wouldn't prevent them from being lonely. I had known many married people who were lonely because their spouse couldn't fulfill their every need. I told them they needed to have some completeness within themselves. If not, they would just drain any relationship they had because they would always look to their partner for fulfillment.

I never knew that moment would hit my life. Prior to my Ken's death, although we were married , I enjoyed having my alone time, or what I called my "Me Time." I always believed and still do believe that you have to learn how to enjoy yourself first and then you can truly bring joy to someone else life. Although these were the beliefs I had, I was still faced with being alone at that moment.

Once my errands were finished, I started by calling my daughter who had a husband and a family of her own. She didn't answer the phone. She would normally call me right back, but not this day. Next up was my daughter-in-law but she and my son had plans of their own. The calling continued and it almost felt like a conspiracy because no one answered, or if they did, they already were in the midst of doing something. I said to myself, okay, well, if they're too busy for me, then surely, I can call a friend and treat her to lunch. Nothing I did worked this beautiful Saturday morning. It was complete silence on that day.

Tears began to stream down my eyes and at that very moment, I felt lonely. I never remember feeling like this before. I was now faced with the reality that my life had changed forever. After all, I did experience a great loss. Why not just give in to a life of silence and hiding?

Why should I continue to trust and believe in God since he allowed my husband to die without any warning to me? I thought at least I could have prepared my heart. Well, there you go, my five minutes of pity that God gave me. I often tease and say to God, "Come on now can I have more than five minutes of pity before I get up and fight for my healing and deliverance."

The question is this; will you really be prepared for that kind of life-changing event? The answer is no. When I thought about how life would have been if God would have shown me ahead of time that this would happen, would I have really been prepared? After all, I had been married for 25 years with a friendship even longer. We had a good strong marriage without separation and we not only had fun together, but we enjoyed each other's company most of the time (lol). I would have fought with everything in me to keep him around.

As I continued to ride and cry, trying to find somewhere to go, God spoke to my heart and asked, "What does Lisa want?" I was totally offended. I began to answer out loud. I said, "What do you mean what do I want and who am I?". That was like saying I had sacrificed and put my life and dreams on hold for my family and that I may have lost a part of myself along the way.

Although I didn't like the questions, I realized I had put some of my dreams on hold. Now, to be honest with you, if I had to choose between keeping my spouse here or pursuing a dream, I would have chosen to take care of my spouse, especially if it was impossible to do both at the same time. After all, I had a good strong, and stable marriage. My husband and I were in ministry together. He was the pastor and I was a minister and counselor. God brought to my remembrance that I always told the church that the bulk of my ministry was outside of the walls of the church. Marinate on that.

The words started again and I began to speak aloud and say, "what do you mean what does Lisa want?. I have had what I wanted and now he's gone and my life has forever changed. It was still just a few months after my husband passed when I was having these thoughts, so I know bitterness was trying to settle in, but God brought to my remembrance the conversation I had with him while on the hospital floor when they pronounced him dead. When I fell to the floor crying, my first sentence was, "God, what are you doing? I don't understand". The very next sentence out of my mouth was for God to make me better and not bitter.

I've always been nurturing and liked helping and motivating others and I knew if I was bitter, I wouldn't be able to help anyone. I told God at that moment, if he saw me through this, I would help others deal with their grief. What I didn't under-stand in the car that day was that God was trying to help me. I had to make the decision to surrender to his way of getting me through this. There wasn't a bypass or a shortcut. This journey was mine with God every step of the way.

Realization set in that the only way to get through it was to embrace a new life. I then understood the question of what it was that I wanted. As I continued to drive, the tears were still coming but a smile was also trying to come through and I began to ponder over my life and ask myself the same questions. As quickly as I asked myself the questions, so many thoughts came to me and a hint of excitement was in the air. I became excited at the thought of being able to have a choice of how I wanted to live the rest of my life and what I wanted to do with it. I had the choice of living better than this crisis was giving me or to just existing. This was my opportunity to embrace my next chapters.

I then understood why no one was available to me that day. It was a defining moment for me and I had to find my own path. During times like these, so many people have so many opinions about how you should live your life after such a loss. I heard so many different things like; don't do anything for a year, don't go anywhere, and don't go back to work. People were saying you are vulnerable, so just don't do anything. Well, trust me, during the first few months, I couldn't do much of anything. It took every ounce of strength just to get out of bed. I couldn't eat or sleep. I was just drained and I lost about thirty pounds quickly. Something I could never do when I tried at other times. LOL!

I would pick up the bible and try to read it but I would open it and then close it. I would try to pray, but the only words I could get out while bursting into tears was," God help me, this feels unbearable." I told God there was no way I could get through this on my own and that I needed him to see me through this. This pain felt indescribable but day after day, I realized it was unbearable in my own strength, but God's strength would rise up in me.

This day was my day of having a new life and embracing it. I made a decision to live life to the fullest instead of just existing. I decided not to check out on life but to embrace more possibilities in life. I could have easily checked out not physically but mentally by being depressed and barely existing. I see people on a daily basis who seem to have no hope and just exist with no real purpose for living. Those are the people I want to reach out to and let them know life isn't over and it can begin again as long as you have breathed in your body.

Although I was still very much wounded, I accepted my new life. For the next few days I would just ponder and think of the new things I wanted to do in life. My life was being changed once again and it didn't mean I wouldn't grieve anymore; it didn't mean I wouldn't hurt or cry. It just simply meant I could have a new life with many new chapters in it. I had to decide to change with it.

Giving in to my circumstances has never been an option for me. Anytime I would go through tough times in life, I would always try to cry and have a pity party for myself, but it never worked for me. It's like a voice would always say okay, now you've cried and pouted, now get up and fight some more. I would then laugh and tell God, that it'sunfair that he made me this way. I wondered why I couldn't feel sorry for myself like others did. I realized a long time ago that's just not who I am. Yes, I have my moments of crying just like the next person but I have strength on the inside that says get up and fight another day.

Writing this book was one of the new chapters in my life so that I can help others through their time of grief and let the world know that you don't have to give up or check out of life because of it. Yes, it hurts and it can be depressing, but you don't have to camp out there. There is help available for you. During this time professional and spiritual help can be great tools for healing. Just please remember healing is a process.

It doesn't mean years later, a moment won't hit you and you begin to cry, but you can decide never to get stuck in that moment. Crank up your camper, pick up your tent, and move. The campground of staying stuck is closed here. We have to realize we were creating for a bigger purpose than just ourselves. I had to get through this not only for my y family and me but to make an impact on many people's lives just by sharing my story with them.

Define your life today and open yourself up to new possibilities. Don't continue to live in the hurt of the past but embrace the present and future opportunities. It's called new Grace and mercy daily. Think of some of the things in life you've always wanted to do and start with that. Even if it's something small, start with that and whatever you start, FINISH it! That's one of the things I've learned through this process is to finish what I started. One of the things I started years ago was college, so when I turned 45, I went back and got my Master's Degree. Look at God!

It's not too late to have a Defining Moment. Don't let others tell you how to live your life. Get your pen and pad out and write down some of the accomplishments you would like to achieve and begin to research and find out what steps you need to take in order to achieve them.

So now I can answer the question that was asked of me. Who am I? I am God's chosen one and I'm more than a conqueror and nothing can separate me from the love of God, not even death. Since I didn't allow death to make me check out on life, then it can't stop me from being who I was created to be. Death no longer had its sting over me because the sting was already taken for me.

Who am I, you asked again? I am the one who sits here writing this book to encourage my readers to get up from the blow that life has dished out. It may be death, divorce, loss of a job, a loved one, or a host of many other losses. You may not have all the answers, but please realize in this life some questions will never be answered.

Get up and celebrate life! The fact that you're breathing means you have a second chance to improve the quality of your life and the life of others.

Although this seemed to happen without any warning, I also knew God didn't allow it just to hurt me or punish me. I realized I had to open my heart and allow the healing process to begin. I also realized that once I opened up that I could get through this devastating time in my life. I began to see that life wasn't over for me, but it was a new beginning, no matter how painful it was at this moment. I suddenly remembered a few days before my husband died. He looked at me and told me to always remember that I am a strong woman. I accepted it even though I had no idea of what was to come.

"The past cannot be changed.
The future is yet in your power."
- Hugh White

CHAPTER TWELVE
STRONG-WISER-BETTER

Older people have often said If it doesn't kill you, it will make you strong. Although you sometimes feel like dying or giving up, you must know that God is making you stronger for his divine purpose if you will allow it. The only person who can stop you is the man or woman in the mirror.

When you feel like throwing in the towel that's when God is carrying you. So many times, we read the footprint poem without really knowing what it means. When God allows that wilderness experience to come into your life, it's then when you feel hopeless and lost, as if you can't go on. Day after day and week after week you stop and think "How in the world did I make it to this point, at that very moment, you realize God has held you close in his arms.

God uses what seems to be the darkest point in our lives to push us past our limits so that we can experience his supernatural power in our lives. When it seems that he has allowed the most important thing or person on earth to be taken away from us is when you are empty enough to clearly hear from him. You have to want to move forward. God and no one else can do it without your participation.

I have been ministering now for 20 years or so. Anytime I've been at a weak point in life and I continue to trust God through it, he gives me an unusual anointing and strength, when we surrender to his process. Every time I opened my mouth to speak, he amazes me with the words that he gives me. Most of them weren't in my notes. LolBefore I speak, I ask God to help me to decrease so that he can use me, but some time ago I changed my prayer. I begin to tell God to glorify himself through me and now I'm experiencing just that. God continues to amaze me.

A few days had passed after my husband died. I was hurting so bad but I asked God to help me become better and not bitter. Here's why; throughout life, I have always had a passion for helping people in many ways such as; family and marriage counseling and even just being a good friend. I knew that if I allowed this to make me bitter then I wouldn't be able to help anyone and that has always been important to me. I have always known that one of the gifts that God gave me was to motivate and encourage others even if I was going through trials or troubles. It has always been a type of therapy for me to help others because somehow it made me feel better about any situation I was going through.

I can truly tell you that I'm stronger, wiser, and much better than I was before and that's all because I decided to fight back and give back to others. Instead of camping out at Pity Party Island. I made sure I told family and friends that they had to treat me the same way they treated me before this tragedy. My

family is a very big family. We have always been very enter-
taining when we all get together, so this remained important
to me.

I knew if I allowed the pity party then I would never get over
this. Since my husband was so close to my parents and my
siblings, of course, we would have times when we were together
that we all sat in my mom's living room and everyone in the
room would be crying. We decided to allow ourselves to cry but
we also made a pack to celebrate his life by remembering the
impact he made in this world and how he made us laugh.

There were also days that I just decided I'm not sitting around
crying all day. One day my baby sister (Yolanda) called me and
asked if I was coming to our parent's house for dinner. Sunday
was the day of the week that we all came over with our families
and ate Sunday dinner together. This time she sounded really
sad on the phone but I decided to go anyway. When I got in the
door her face was all scrunched up. I could look at her face and
tell she was missing Ken.

This was also sad for me but I had decided that I wasn't having
a depression party that day. I hugged her briefly and kissed her
cheek and whispered to her, "I choose not to be sad today so if
you're going to stay that way then I'm going to leave". She first
looked and rolled her eyes at me in disbelief (Lol) but changed
her expression.

I explained to her that grief hurts worse than any heartache I
ever felt, and comes in waves without warning. Sometimes the
day may start out joyful then out of nowhere the tears begin
to flow. Many days it was a fight but I would look in the
mirror and say, "no I won't be sad today instead I'm going to
celebrate life." After all, I still had to be thankful that I was

allowed one more day to live and make an impact on someone else life.

It may sound crazy to some but through this process, since I didn't allow depression or disparity to lord over me, I have become much more INTENTIONAL in life and how I want to live it.. This too can be your testimony. Come on reach deep within yourself and find your strength because we all have some if we will allow it to come out.

They that wait upon the LORD chall renew their strength; they chall mount up with wings of eagles; they chall run, and not be weary; and they chall walk and not faint. -ISAIAH 40:31

CHAPTER THIRTEEN
STILL STANDING

The critics looked and watched to see if I would crumble. Some of them were praying and rooting for me to get up again. Then others were saying, "Now let's see what she's going to do now"Believe it or not even though I've been through this tragedy some people were hoping this would keep me down. If the truth be told they have always been jealous of whom they thought you were so this gives them a smirk. I know this sounds crazy to you right now and you want to think everyone in the world has compassion for what you are going through. As sad as it may sound some of the people in close proximity have these thoughts.

Growing up people always told me I was strong and I never knew why. As I continued to live life and went through many obstacles there were people who admired me and then there were the pretenders. The pretenders are those around you who think they would love to be you because they think your life was always good. They didn't know the trials and tribulations that came along with your journey. They just saw something in you that they didn't understand. The whisperers think they can wear your shoes until they realized once size never fits all. My shoes may be too tight for you to walk int. It's best to stay in your own lane so that you won't have a collision.

When you have a purpose for living no matter what comes your way you will get up again although some people like you better when you're down. These are the people who feel lowly about themselves and in order to make themselves feel better, they wish you would fall down and stay there even in a time like this.

As I always say," The devil is a liar." Life will knock you down sometime but that doesn't mean it was a TKO. God can turn a knockout into a victory. It was a punch that knocked me down for a while but then I realized God created me for greatness to make a difference in so many lives. I slowly began to get some strength. There were still many days of pain and heartache but there were also rays of hope, a glimpse of life, and a strength to fight back like never before. I knew I was still needed by my children, family, friends, and maybe even my frenemies.

People that have never been through it can't possibly under-stand what's best for you. They may feel sad because it's their loved one too but they will never be able to comprehend your loss so stop trying to make them understand. Just do what it takes to use your crutches and learn to walk again. No matter what you do or how you do it people will talk so, get up and give them something worth talking about.

I had to start out with baby steps. If you must hold on to some-thing or someone such as a friend or family member then grab a hold. If you find that song that gives you healing through the music then play until it won't play anymore. When the song stops playing then find another one and move on to the next song for the next phase.

It seems as if God would give me a song to lean on for a few weeks then change to another one. During this time, I would turn the music up loud and just dance while I was crying. I danced through my tears because I was dancing to God's beat of how he was carrying me through and walking alongside me.

I would put on my music whether gospel or soothing jazz and I would dance in the presence of God. I would literally be dancing, praying, and talking to God all at the same time. While dancing the tears would be rolling but the dance would go on for a while. When the dance was over, I would feel as if I was ready to fight a little more and to live another day.

One of my forever songs during this process and even today was by Marvin Sapp calle; Rivers Flowing.

During this process forget about the naysayers who try to tell you it's too soon to do this or you shouldn't do that. Find out what works for you and for the healing process to begin. Nobody can tell you what it is. This is something strictly between you and God. The only thing that you can do on your own is to make a decision to live again. People won't understand and they don't have to because it's your life and only you can walk this one out. I've always walked in my own lane because I will trip and fall trying to walk or run in another person's lane.

It's a reason running tracks have lanes if everyone tried to stay in the same lane, they would trip over the feet of the others. That would become a disaster on the track. Everyone has their own assigned lanes in life so please don't try to be anyone else but the person God created you to be. My lane won't work for you. Neither will yours work for me.

As each day passed, I felt stronger and I knew I would make it. Although I would still have some bad days, they were getting less frequent. I was filling my heart and mind with positive thoughts and words and I was taking action in my life. I would begin to look in the mirror and say to myself, "you can do this". I never alluded to myself as if I wouldn't hurt anymore because I've always tried to be real with myself. What I began to say to myself and to God was this; This pain feels agonizing, unbearable and my heart is totally broken, but I not only can get through this but I have to.

Someone is looking for hope. Someone is looking to see that I can go through a time like this and stand up again and live because it gives them hope. Our trials are never just about us.

Whatever you do, don't do it for a show because that will lead to a breakdown but do it for yourself and to reclaim your life. It's not about you and it's not about me but it's about helping someone else who feels like they can't take the pressure of life anymore. It's about the little girl whose mother died when she was in the prime of her teen years. It's about the son whose dad left him when he was just beginning to learn how to be a man. It's about the woman or man who's gone through the death of a marriage and feel hopeless. It's about someone who lost their livelihood and all their belongings. You see someone has lost everything, their, house, the car, and a threat of losing the kids.

If they could just see someone who has been through a life crisis that hurts beyond measure stand up again this may give them the inspiration to try again. They may see your tears but you're still trying to stand up again. Start taking baby steps and go outside to look at the sun. This is the infancy stage of recovery. Next instead of trying to stand you begin to walk and wobble a little bit further.

You're in the toddler stage of your healing. You open the door this time and you decide to bring a chair out with you because it's a beautiful day and the weather seems just right. The next day maybe a day to stay inside because it seems you have a setback. Just know this is a normal process as long as you don't get stuck.

A few days passed and I was walking without the wobble. My steps were beginning to line up. I got into the car and I begin to drive again. I was growing and moving. While driving I began to see life a little differently than before. There was a ray of light and it was giving me such a peace that surprised even me. There was now a little bit of excitement birthing forth.

I kept dancing in the rain. I didn't stop walking or moving forward, because I now have a new direction. I begin to realize I've made it this far and I began to think I could make it a little bit further.

Whatever you do continue to speak life to yourself and know that you can win. Get up go outside and walk again. It's your time to shine and you can stand up with your head held high because God is about to take you to new heights since you didn't give up. Go ahead and take a few more steps into your new chapters of life.

Get up look in the mirror and tell yourself you can make it and you will get through this because you weren't created to fail. The very fact that you're able to stand up again puts you in a better position than ever before. You're in a greater position because you're taking steps through this storm. Although the enemy wanted to use this to defeat you, he didn't win. You're breathing and moving and you still have your being. So, get up, get out, and stand tall because you're about to conquer old fears, dream new dreams, and discover a part of yourself that you never knew before.

You were counted out and all eyes are on you but don't get caught up in whose watching you. Just remember who's carrying you until you can stand up again. If you weren't meant to live beyond this loss then you would have died when you got the news. There were still others who said they would be there for you no matter what but they turned their backs on you because you didn't do things their way. That's okay this was your season to change into the new person you now see in the mirror.

Jilted Stand
I felt Jilted and hurt beyond what you see
But my trust stayed in God for complete victory
I couldn't do it on my own nor did I try
The only thing I could do was barely get by
So, I transferred it from hand to hand
Because now was the time for God's masterplan
I was too weak and had no strength at all
But God came through and I'm now standing tall
So I understand the saying; I don't look like what I've been through
After it was all said and done God came to my rescue
Lisa T

CHAPTER FOURTEEN
DANCE

Some didn't understand how I could praise my God so quickly after my husband passed. After all, God had given me a good strong marriage for all those years without any separation, and seemingly without notice, he was gone.

All I can say is that this painful life-changing event gave me a deeper reverence for God. I understood now more than ever God created me to glorify him. As I turned the music on the tears began to flow, but I began to dance in the presence of the Lord. Rivers of living water seemed to be flowing out of me and I felt totally free to praise God almighty without restraint.

As I danced, he softly spoke to my heart, assuring me that everything will get better and that he has plans for my life that will far exceed my imagination. He will replace all the pain and despair that I was feeling with joy. He then seemed to quiet my heart while I continued to dance . When I would slow down my heart told me to keep dancing because God would be with me forever.

During this time, I was encouraged through songs. As I listened to the song by Maurette Brown Clark; It Ain't Over, it says, it's not over until God says it's over, and to keep fighting, keep believing, keep praying until the Victory is won. I literally understood that God's strength was truly made perfect in my weakness because without him I would have failed.

With each passing day, I was getting stronger. I refused to give in to the feelings of despair and depression. Somehow, I knew that God would bring me through this, even in the midst of this indescribable, agonizing pain in my heart.

I returned to my dancing and I felt like I was 16 years old dancing without any care in the world. I felt myself in the arms of God and he was carrying me through this time in my life. I continually thank him for his goodness.

Giving him thanks in everything is what I did with each new day. In spite of it all, my God was and still is good to me. Once again, he causes me to triumph over any plans the devil had for me.

My heart was full of praise for the creator because I knew he never makes mistakes even when we don't understand. He still leads me to a prosperous, prominent life. He promises never to leave me or forsake me and I now know it to be true.

As I danced, I realize more and more every day it was not about me. The joy of the Lord was truly my strength. In his presence is fullness of joy. My heart feels totally connected with his. God truly is the wind beneath my wings and I love him more every day.

Your dance may be different from mine but whatever your dance is just do it until you find comfort in it. Your dance could be a long walk in the park, going to the gym for a workout, listening to a motivational tape, or going out with friends. No matter what your dance is just dance to the tune until you find inner peace and comfort. This may be the very outlet that gets you moving forward in life. Turn the music on and dance, after all, you have to get up sometime or you will just be existing without purpose. Learn to dance in the rain.

CHAPTER FIFTEEN
A NEW DAY

On this particular morning, I woke up with new air-breathing in me. The sun was shining bright & beautiful. I decided to get up and take advantage of the moment I was in. In life, we have to decide to make the most of each day because we will never see that day again.

The mere fact that you're breathing says' this is a new day and I can start afresh. What does this freshness or this newness mean to you? It seemed that life had dealt me a hand without any winning cards. People may have done you wrong, your bank account may be in the red and your car may be a lemon. Yet and still, you woke up today. You have the advantage of starting over right at this very moment. It all starts in your mind. You need to have a purpose in your heart today to make a change.

This can be your turning point. Who told you that you can't begin again at your age? Who told you that you're too old to go back to school or start that new business? Who told you that you're too young to make a change? Don't listen to the lies the world is telling you.

Make a decision right now. I dare you to run with this new day. Are you afraid of success? What will stop you from conquering? Who told you not to fly? Well, I'm telling you to take a deep breath. Do it again and again until you feel the freshness of the day.

Now begin to meditate on a fresh start. You have to see it in your mind before it can manifest. Go after it with all of your might. That's exactly what I did while leaning on the Lord, and acknowledging and asking for divine direction.

I believe every person born was born with a purpose designed by God. Regardless of how you came about you came because of God's purpose for your life. There is a shining moment in your life, there is a moment of time in your life when you must stand up and stand out. At this moment your background or where you came from won't matter. All that will matter is that you move with intention.

When it's your time to shine, it's your time. Nothing can stop it. Not your background, race, friends, teachers, or any of the naysayers. As long as your mind is made up nothing or no one will be able to stop you from shining. This life-changing event wasn't meant to hurt me or you. Although we won't understand everything in this life, we can have a say over the life we live while we have breath in our bodies.

Each day is a new day so why sit here and die? When one dies physically, they're no longer here, but if you die in your spirit then you're already defeated. I'm not saying it's easy but it can be done. I'm doing it right now because I refused to just exist so

I decided to take my life and move forward with it. I would love for the person reading this to move forward . Let's get up, clean up, wash your face and let's move forward.

Decide what you want out of life at this very moment. Stop reliving the pain and look to the future. You can no longer live in the past because you can't undo what's already happened. You have to decide how you want your life to play out from this point forward. It's your new day so make the most of it.

Think about some of the goals you use to have. Was it to finish your education in order to put yourself in a better position financially? Was it to get in better physical condition by eating better and exercising? Do you want to travel the world? All of these are good things to do but remember none of them will fall into your lap. You have to start somewhere. You don't have to start with the biggest thing but you do have to start with something. Sometimes it's better to start with the smaller goals and complete them because it gives you the feeling of empowerment. This gives you a feeling like all things are possible and now you're ready for the next goal.

My new day began years ago writing in my online journal that turned into writing this book. I want to reach anyone that has gotten stuck and paralyzed by their grief. I am doing this by writing and motivating individuals from all walks of life.

I want to reach the hurting people who have had major life-changing events such as the death of a loved one, loss, and even divorce. The list goes on and on. My goal is to encourage others to get the help that's necessary to move on and then pursue their goals, dreams, and visions.

Each new day we get is precious. We have to decide to live our life to the fullest and make an impact on the lives of others.

If I never have a million dollars to leave my family, I pray that the life I lived, the lessons I've taught, and most of all my character will give them the wisdom to live a prosperous and fulfilled life, that'sfull of God-given wisdom. My new day tells others they can make it through the storms of life so don't give up. My new day began years ago because I had to re-discover myself. I started by finishing the projects I once started such as finishing my education and writing this book.

My new days always began with me thanking God for allowing me to see another day. Next, my main focus was and still is to help someone each day. Even if it's by way of a phone call giving someone some encouraging words. I may send out an inspirational text or email but I'm compelled to help someone have a new day.

I know you may be hurting right now because your loved one has died but get up life isn't over for you. Get up and live again. You may have gone through some form of abuse as a child or an adult and you may be free from it physically but you're allowing it to control you emotionally. There was a divorce and you had no say in the matter. Your spouse decided they wanted out for no apparent reason.

It's not your fault so get up, get yourself some help and call a friend or a family member and tell them how you feel. If counseling is needed then go ahead and make that phone call. Get you a support team and push forward. Don't give the past the power to stunt your future growth. Don't allow the pain to decide how you're going to live. The fact that you're reading this book means you survived it even if you don't feel like a survivor. You have another chance today is a new day.

Don't let your past dictate your future. The future is in your hands now, so what will you do with it? Will you allow your circumstances to rule your life? Or, will you get up and fight and take your life back? I hope you chose the second one. There is hope for your future and you're the only one who can stop it. It won't be easy but it can be done. If one door closes look for the next open door. Remember for every no there is still a yes out there waiting for you. Discouragement will come but don't let it stop you. It's okay to fail on your way up. Failure is only failure if you never try. Never trying to look for opportunities to better yourself is a failure.

If it's the death of a loved one, grieve, cry, scream or yell but know you can get through it and live a prosperous life again. Find whatever help you need then move forward because getting stuck in grief won't bring your loved one back.

If it's the loss of a job, get up and look for another one. Even if it means you need to further your education get up and do it. After you've done your part, go ahead and update your resume and walk into your open door. Or better yet if there's not an opened door yet, then create one for yourself. Dream again and start your own company.

Grief and loss from someone or something you loved isn't the final word over your life. If your spouse/significant other didn't want you anymore or didn't see your value in their life, then move on because someone else will. It all starts with loving yourself and knowing that you're a precious gift from God. Just because the person you loved didn't know how to appreciate the gift and open it up doesn't mean it wasn't a gift. When someone chooses to walk away from your life, take a deep breath and move on.

Each new day is a gift. Sometimes we're given gifts and don't know their worth until it's too late. Then someone else will get the gift sobe thankful for it and do everything possible to continually unwrap the gift and love it and it will grow stronger and stronger.

Now look in the mirror and ask yourself, who am I and what do I want in life? Then be prepared to have the answers. Go write down your goals, dreams, and your visions and start working on them.

I know you can do it because I stand here as an example to you and I encourage you to get up and LIVE AGAIN!!!

Come on let's run together. Don't worry about the cards that were dealt to you but learn how to play your hand. The sun can and will shine again!

CHAPTER SIXTEEN
NEW EYES

I was reminded of Bishop Paul Morton's song; I Am What You See. Some of the lyrics say "Open my eyes help me believe I am what you see. This helped me to ask God to open my eyes even more so that I could see myself as he sees me.

We're not only God's creation but we're very special to him and he loves us unconditionally. We should never think too highly of ourselves but he definitely didn't intend for us to think low of ourselves at all.

I began to ask God for new eyes, to see past the hurt and obstacles of life. You may be asking the question; can I possibly get over this? Will my heart stay broken forever? Do dreams really come true? Can I start all over again?

As long as you live on this earth change is inevitable. It allows you to see what you're made of. God called each of us to win. We have to purpose in our hearts to win. The victory starts in our minds. We have to first decide to overcome the obstacles of life. That doesn't mean you can change everything but you can change the way you view life and make the necessary adjustments with God's help.

It's a matter of choice. Will we speak life or will we continually speak damnation? We clearly have a choice. Can we see past the wall that has been built? Or can we dream again? This time with a purpose. We have to purpose, plan and prepare to win. Nothing will just appear at your front door. You must be INTENTIONAL!

Remember along the way winning may not look like we want it to look. Remember this; if God is the one who altered the plan, you have no choice but to accept it.

It's time to lace up your sneakers and run. We all have some wilderness experiences. There's always a lesson to be learned to make us stronger. Stop waiting for a handout because one day no one will be handing anything out. In the long run, if you stay in the handout line it will handicap you. You will never meet up with purpose by staying in that line. One day you can be the one with the solution instead of the problem. Allow God to open your eyes. God wants to clear up your vision.

I ask you today "Can you see yourself going from that weight to a healthier you? Do you see the diploma on the wall? Or better yet can you see that GED turning into a degree? Remember this; with men things are impossible but with God all things are possible.

I was at a loss for words and void of any type of understanding as to why this happened to me. This seem to be so surreal and each and every day I would create a story in my mind of the doctor calling me back saying they had made a mistake. Only this day never came. I was faced with losing my spouse after 25 years without any warning of it.

Although I was planning the funeral I was still in disbelief and still awaiting that call from the hospital saying they had made a mistake. The phone call never came and it was months later that I rehearsed that same scenario in my head even though I was beginning to function again. I held on to that imaginary phone call. Months would pass me by and although I was getting out of the house and doing things that needed to be done, I still had hopes that this was all a mistake.

I thought this pain would never leave and I couldn't imagine life without my spouse. We had a good strong marriage and if any obstacles came along the way we worked through them all, so how could this happen to my family?

One day I had to stop asking why and even rehearsing my scenario. I asked God to give me a new set of eyes. A new vision, and a purpose that was bigger than me.

With my new set of eyes came this book that started out as journaling from years ago. My new vision also included doing grief recovery work to help others to Live and not merely exist because there is a difference.

Vision

Dear God, it's me
Right now, Lord, I can't see
I'm throwing in the towel of doing it on my own
I heard a voice say you're still on the throne
You can work miracles and have all power in your hands
If I will only trust and believe in your greater plans
Can you help me to trust you beyond what I see?
Please open my eyes and help me believe
Dear Lord, once again it's your child, yes, it's me
Help me believe I am what you see.
Lisa T

CHAPTER SEVENTEEN

THE PROCESS

My process was uncomfortable for me at first. I had to go to another church and sit down without doing anything but listening to the word. I later understood why. I'm a natural helper even when and if I'm going through a trial or stressful life event.

This was God's way of having me do absolutely nothing for anyone else. This was a time for much self-care which I found to be totally necessary even though it was uncomfortable.

It felt like I deserted the church because I had to leave. At the time I didn't know how to explain in-depth why. I did tell them I had to sit down to heal. In hindsight, I would have definitely done things differently. I just knew that I was fading away if I kept going the way I was going. My body was trying to shut down as well so I had to heal in order to LIVE.

When finally coming to grips with my world being shaken to the core, I realized that my process was a journey of self-discovery with a whole lot of self-care. This was necessary so that I could show up in my next season of life and be present for myself first, my children and grandchildren. Yes, our children were fully grown and married. But they still needed me here.

I had to be intentional with my life and the fact that I was still here and wanted to be here on this earth. I knew God wasn't through with me and the purposes he had and still has for me to fulfill.

Make no mistake this was the most painful, heart-wrenching, and devasting event that I'd ever gone through. I cried daily while lying on the floor in agony with a fainting voice I would say things like;

- God, I don't understand
- This feels unbearable
- He was pastoring and trying to live what he preached
- God our children are hurting
- The church is hurting
- What am I supposed to do now?
- I feel like I can't go on
- This is too hard

Somehow after all of that my hands would raise without even trying. After all of the questions and thoughts the words that came out of my mouth were; "God I still love and trust you."

I also told God there was no way I could get through this process. I told him if he wanted me to get through this then he would have to carry me through. He did just that!

The process was different but necessary. This type of healing was between me and the creator. The process was different each day. God was literally giving me different avenues to soothe and comfort me while crying and hurting.

Listen! Every time I tried to pick up the bible and read it, I would just close it, but the word was in me. I would just simply speak aloud the word that was already hidden in my heart. Yes, it really works! It's not a quick fix but a process. If you speak the word and apply it to your life, and circumstances it will eventually quicken within you.

In no way does this mean any type of magic or name it and claim it. What it meant for me is that when I spoke the truth of his word then it would heal my life even if it wasn't in the way I wanted it to. We have to realize God's plans for our lives are so much better than we can ever imagine.

We may not understand it, but if we begin to trust the process we will walk, talk, and move differently than we ever have before.

One month God would put a song on my heart and I would be crying and dancing in his presence. That song would be played every day until he gave me a new one. Dancing was a part of my healing daily even while the tears were flowing

Throughout my journey, God gave me different books to read and they weren't necessarily on grieving. I learned to flow with God's rhythm which meant total surrender.

What my process taught me was to continually walk in my OWN LANE! I can't do it like anyone else. I didn't listen to the super saints or the naysayers. I unapologetically followed God leading and guidance. That's why I'm here to encourage, uplift, and inspire others to move forward because life isn't over after loss.

Trust the process! Your new journey begins now!

Thessalonians 5:18

In everything give thanks: for this is the will of God in Christ Jesus concerning you.

CHAPTER EIGHTEEN
HEALING TIME

My phone kept ringing from the saints of course. Message after message with words like; you just have to pray and have faith. Well, surely you haven't paid attention to me over the years, because that's how I live through prayers and continued faith. What a cliché!

What happens when prayer and faith seemingly aren't stopping the excruciating pain your heart is feeling? What happens when you can't pick up your bible to read? What happens when your body responds to grief with sadness, anger & sickness?

My doctor looked me in my face and said" I know you're a minister, I know you're a woman of faith. Now I'm telling you as a doctor who believes in God that you need to sit down and heal." He went on to tell me that my body is shutting down because of the heaviness of grieving and trying to be there for everyone else including the church.

That lead to a series of doctor visits because I developed stomach ulcers that could have quickly turned into cancer according to my doctors. He said it had already permanently affected my vocal cords, and esophagus. I lost 30 lbs. in less than 2 months because I couldn't eat or sleep.

I never had blood pressure issues before, but my blood pressure was dangerously low because my body wasn't getting any sleep or rest. I woke up every two hours for months.

Now I said all of that to tell you to sit down when you need to or your body will force you to do so. So needless to say, I had to tune out the Super Saints and sit down and allow my healing journey to take its course.

This was a time when God didn't want me preaching, teaching, or speaking as I normally had. It was time for me to do my self-care God's way.

So many times, we listen to church folks that say just keep preaching, and keep going. Well, one thing that's true still to this day I accepted and walked in my calling and that will never change. I just have the wisdom of God to know that he wants us whole and healthy so that we can continually do his work.

I made the best decision for me at the time and that was to listen to the doctors. My PCP (Dr. John Hackenberg) and my Otolaryngologist-ENT (Dr. Charles Greene) from Jacksonville, FL worked together to help me get well. Dr. Greene would do his part medically and after advising me he would reach for my hand. He never let me leave his office without asking God to heal and cover me. Upon taking their advice I sat down to allow the healing to begin.

My journey may have looked different from yours but I have always believed in walking in my own lane, and doing it how I was being led to do so.

Church, pastors, first ladies, ministers, and leaders please take the time to heal and stop doing what you think the people want. If you're not whole, how can you effectively lead? This holds true for grieving of any kind such as death, divorce, loss, and a host of other painful life events.

Stop trying to be a superhero. God made you human. He felt any and every emotion we can feel. This doesn't mean you've lost your faith. It simply means you were strong enough to take a seat and HEAL!

So many leaders today preach powerful sermons and then go into a drak room and are depressed because they haven't dealt with their grief or mental health. This doesn't mean you have a mental diagnosis. It simply means you need to do some much needed self-care so that it don't turn into mental health or suicidal thoughts or actions. Now let that marinate.

All throughout my life in almost every arena people have considered me as a strong person. I accepted that I was indeed strong. I was also strong enough to know that at this moment in time I was weak.

Real strength knows when to take a rest until you're able to pick the baton back up again. I cried and cried but I totally gave myself over to becoming whole, healed, and recovered.

God allows us to go through our losses not to hurt us but he will definitely use it so that we can show others what's possible. There's someone that doesn't have the faith or endurance that you have. They may need to see that we can go through something horrific and get through it. You don't have to be a super-hero. Trust that Almighty God can help us to stand again.

It all began with me taking the time to sit down and heal so that I could stand up again to tell the world of my life-changing moment that took the wind out of me.

To also let the grieved and bereaved know that even though we may feel Jilted, we can make it through. We have to lean, depend, and cast our cares on God. Even though it felt like I was lifeless, morning kept coming! Which meant the rest of my story was still unwritten and I had a say in what was next for me with God directing me.

I'm speaking to everyone on the planet, but to the spiritual leaders please know that your calling doesn't change but maybe the platform will. This doesn't apply to everyone but be open to your new chapters and a fresh wind.

Be open to new ventures, ideas, next chapters, and most of all living again instead of barely existing.

Thank God I don't look like what I've been through
You too can have this testimony
It's time to heal and recover

CHAPTER NINETEEN
INTENTIONAL

G rief was never intended to be a life sentence. It's a process that you can absolutely work through. Moving forward is attainable and achievable. However, it will never happen without your full participation.

Put one foot out of the bed and then the next one. Stand up, get up, and decide to show up for yourself today.

Look in the mirror and tell yourself that you were created for a purpose bigger than you. As the psalmist said, you were fearfully and wonderfully made.

God took his time to design you for his purpose. You are not your own!

Yes, in this time of loss and grieving it's hard to feel this. This is the time to cast your cares on the creator and know that he can handle it and get you through it. There is nothing too hard for God.

Just remember in order for faith to be activated you have to participate. Nothing will drop out of the sky besides, water, rain, sleet, or snow so you must surrender to the process.

Decide to be present. This doesn't mean you won't have any more bad days. It just means you must not retreat or throw in the towel. Cry if you must but after the tears get up and determine in your heart that you will get better.

This is a time of self-discovery for the man or woman in the mirror. So, I ask you what do you want out of life? How do you see yourself? What are some of your dreams and aspirations? Who are you?

Begin to answer these questions. Remember to think before you answer these questions. Think of this for yourself alone. Just simply reflect on some of the things in the past that you wanted for yourself before your life took another course.

For those that were married and now widowed or the once married but now divorced person remember you're still an individual. Many people often say they want a mate to complete them. I say you must be complete within yourself and then two complete people can and should complement one another's life

Your individuality is important. If you're not whole you will never have the full life that was intended for you. This is a time of discovery and new opportunities.

Embrace your new chapters. Life is full of uncertainties but equally full of new opportunities that are waiting on you to show up. Show up for yourself!

This all starts with changing the way you see life. You can choose to see it negatively and watch that manifest or you can choose to see positivity and watch the opportunities manifest. It's up to you.

Now, this isn't easy by any means but if you continually retrain/renew your mind it will become easier to shift your mindset.

Whatever loss/losses you've encountered, you can have a better life. This doesn't mean your life wasn't good before. It simply means you now have a new narrative.

Why can't you get a degree or certificate? **Go ahead and take the first step.**

Who said you can't? **With God all things are possible.**

Who lied and said you have to stay sad? **The joy of the Lord can be your strength.**

Did the church tell you to just pray and have faith? **It's okay to seek a counselor as long as it doesn't go against the word of God. Spiritual help is a must but natural help is needed sometimes. It doesn't make you crazy.**

Oh, the devil lied again and said you can't go on? **He's still a liar and the father of lies. Yes, you can!**

The world needs you in it. Be **INTENTIONAL**! I believe in you.

Intentional

The past is the past and can't be changed
But with effort and intention, you can attain.
New life, next chapters is up to you to decide
Put one foot in front of the other and take that stride.
Look in the mirror and say I can WIN!
Because my life's story was already planned.
Before I was formed and before I was birthed
God designed and chose me to come to this earth.
If God said it then it's settled and I know this to be true
Your unwritten story is amazing but it's waiting on you.
Lisa T

CONCLUSION

Grief tends to follow death, divorce, and, many other losses. Some seem to lump it in with what's considered the five stages of dying such as; denial, anger, bargaining, depression, and acceptance. Even though these are considered the stages of dying I certainly went through them all when my husband died. I also went through many responses closely related to grief and loss.

Just like I got through it so can you. The memory of the pain will always be there, but you can live a productive life. The pain can and will lose its sting, but only with your full participation.

The pain of death, divorce, or loss can be heart-wrenching. If you trust in God and surrender then you too can be whole again. Everything we go through in life can be a lesson. Not to hurt us but as a lesson to make us better and usable for God's purpose. We are not our own.

You can make it through this by first confessing it, and surrendering your will to God's way. Faith starts out as a process by first believing and speaking it and then putting in the work.

Choose to become better and never bitter. Sometimes life seems to deal us a bad hand of cards to play. When it's your turn to bid, you don't seem to have any high cards or aces to play. Things may not turn out how we would like them to, but I'm reminded that God's ways are always better than our ways even when we can't see them.

Live on purpose. Don't camp out in the pain of life or you will always miss the purpose. We are not our own. We were all created to live out God's purpose for our life even through the pain. Once we get through it, we can be a testimony to others who aren't nearly as strong as you.

Pull someone else up who seemingly lost their footing and is hanging over a cliff by a thread. Remind them that if you came through, they can also.

Embrace your new season now. New opportunities are awaiting you. Get up, reach forth, and run forward. Your new life is straight ahead.

Always walk in your own lane. Don't try to live like anyone else. Be who you were called to be. That way you won't trip by crossing in another's lane. Be open to change and newness.

Choose joy over sorrow. It's not easy, but definitely possible. Why would you want to live a sad life when there's so much living to do? There's so much you haven't experienced.

If you're having a decent day in the midst of your grief don't allow others to pull you down. Remember this is your process, so don't get stuck in it. You can get through it. It takes surrendering, and a made-up mind to move forward.

Come on let's move forward together in this journey of life. You will begin to discover strengths and desires about yourself that you didn't know were there before.

Although life is full of uncertainties it's also full of possibilities. You can have a better life than you had before. It starts with changing the way you see it.

My purpose is much bigger than the pain that I was feeling. My kids needed me to stay healthy and whole. My grandchildren need me around to impart the wisdom that I was blessed to have that would take them through many generations. There were friends that still needed to see me stand. My family needed my smiling face and positive attitude to see us through some other rough spots in life.

Most of all the world needed to hear my story so that I can touch many lives and encourage others to LIVE and not just exist. Cherish and make the most of each day as if it was your last.

Life is a process of developing into something or someone new at different seasons in our life. Nothing will ever happen by chance. Every experience is used for God's purpose. In every trial, storm, or mishap there's always something to be learned, gained, and used for a greater opportunity than we will ever know.

It's time to move forward and live out your purpose. Instead of camping out on Heartache Boulevard turn the corner onto Destiny Lane keep going and make a right turn on Intentional

Parkway. There you will find your new Life Chapter called *SHIFTING*!

Dance! Turn on your music. Turn it up and just dance!

Don't just exist. LIVE!

ACKNOWLEDGMENTS

It has been said that you should give people their flowers while they're living so here are a few. You each contributed in some way to this book because of your love and support.

My beautiful sisters (Gwen, Faye, Renee, Latonya, & Yolanda) would arrange late-night breakfasts at IHOP. This always included my BFF/Sister (Sherryl Bullock) who's always there. The love and laughter meant everything to me. We had so much fun in the midst of all of our pain. This also includes all of my nieces who were there at late-night breakfast. Sorry nephews, this was a girl's thing (LOL). I love you all.

Auntie Bessie Rodgers, I truly thank you for your love and support always. It was too hard for you to come to the house but as usual, you always show up where it counts.

Denise Tunsil (JD), thank you for moving in with me until the day after the burial. You even offered to stay longer, but I knew this was between me and God. Your love and support helped me so much and I'm forever grateful. I guess that's why we're family twice. Lol

Valerie Brown, you stayed several nights also and continued to show up. You and Ken's bond was truly special with unwavering love. You sensed something was wrong and you showed up that morning. I truly love you and thank you.

Ronald Rodgers, what can I say about you? From day one you were always more than a cousin by marriage. You always treated me as a little sister and you were protective of me even in high school. This time was no different. I truly thank God for all you did for me to take the pressure off.

Robert Bullock II (my double 1st cousin/brother), thank you for always showing up and encouraging me to keep moving forward despite what life threw at me. You have always supported me in word and deeds.

A Special thank you to Marvette Brown and Anita Jones for being there when I could no longer take living in my house when it felt like I was smothering in memories. You did all of the leg work and without my help, you found me an amazing home to live in. I'm forever grateful.

My nephew/son Bernard Brown II & Jairus Brown, although you grieved just as hard as our kids, you have always been there when I needed you and I know it still holds true today.

My nephews Ellis Handy & Robert Ward, you never let a week go by without calling and checking on me. You did this for quite some time and offered your services. I'm forever grateful.

Curtis Clinton, what can I say? Although he was your pastor, he was also like a brother to you. Thank you for being there for every phone call, and anything else I needed.

To Pastor Al and Ida Harris, thank you for showing up when I couldn't preach. Even when I started back preaching, one of you would pop in to support and lift me in prayer. You always answered the phone when I called. You were willing to help in any way you could. I truly thank you both.

Karen Lewis and Gia Burtley Lewis, thank you for the prayers and late-night conversations and confirmations. These priceless moments will forever be in my heart.

To Jean Ribault High School class of '83' words could never express how we have been showing up for each other since graduating high school. God gave us something so precious and rare. We don't just meet up for class reunions, but we show up consistently. I love you all. Thank you to the ones who showed up at my house. You made me laugh during this painful time. You took up a large portion of the church because you had your own section. My heart smiles at the love and support continually.

Carolyn Caldwell, you were there continually. When I would shut down during this time and not answer the phone because of the pain and agony I was in, you still called and showed up. You were there for every part and I truly thank you.

Sherryl Bullock, I could write a book on our genuine love and sisterhood that's forever. You have always been my biggest cheerleader in many areas. You encouraged me to finish this book. You said the world needed to hear it. Words could never express how much you mean to me. Thank you for never leaving my side.

Thanks to all of my sisters-in-law, nieces, nephews, cousins, and every family and friend that showed love and support during this life-changing event.

I'm truly thankful to everyone mentioned and unmentioned for every act of kindness, love, and support. I Love you all.

Last but not least, I thank my Husband Amos, who encouraged, prayed, and uplifted me along the way to finish this book. Your love is truly a gift from God that added to me in abundance with no sorrow. I love you and I thank God for you always.

May God continually bless you.

Made in United States
Orlando, FL
09 July 2022

19564222R00079